GHOSTLY
TALES

About the Author

Billy Roberts (Cornwall, Southwest England) is a registered healer with the National Federation of Spiritual Healers and established the Centre for Psychic and Spiritual Studies and Alternative Therapies in Northern England. He teaches workshops on healing across the UK and is the author of several books, including *The Healing Paw* (HarperCollins). Roberts is also famous throughout the UK as a leading television medium and is currently filming a pilot for the television series *Living with Angels and Demons*. Visit him online at BillyRoberts.co.uk.

To Write the Author

If you wish to contact the author or would like more information about this book, please write to the author in care of Llewellyn Worldwide, and we will forward your request. Both the author and publisher appreciate hearing from you and learning of your enjoyment of this book and how it has helped you. Llewellyn Worldwide cannot guarantee that every letter written to the author can be answered, but all will be forwarded. Please write to:

Billy Roberts
⁒ Llewellyn Worldwide
2143 Wooddale Drive
Woodbury, MN 55125-2989

Please enclose a self-addressed stamped envelope for reply,
or $1.00 to cover costs. If outside the USA, enclose
an international postal reply coupon.

GHOSTLY TALES

POLTERGEISTS, HAUNTED HOUSES, AND MESSAGES FROM BEYOND

BILLY ROBERTS

Llewellyn Publications
Woodbury, Minnesota

First Edition
First Printing, 2014

Book design by Bob Gaul
Cover design by Ellen Lawson
Cover image © iStockphoto.com/8075262/helenecanada
Editing by Ed Day

Llewellyn Publications is a registered trademark of Llewellyn Worldwide Ltd.

Library of Congress Cataloging-in-Publication Data
Roberts, Billy, 1946–
  Ghostly tales: poltergeists, haunted houses, and messages from beyond/Billy Roberts.—First edition.
    pages cm
  ISBN 978-0-7387-3955-7
1. Parapsychology. 2. Occultism. I. Title.
  BF1031.R589 2014
  133.1—dc23
                        2013027480

Llewellyn Publications
A Division of Llewellyn Worldwide Ltd.
2143 Wooddale Drive
Woodbury, MN 55125-2989
www.llewellyn.com

Printed in the United States of America

CONTENTS

INTRODUCTION

I think it's safe to say that everybody loves a good ghost story or spine-chilling tale. There's nothing quite like curling up on the settee in front of the fire, or sitting up in bed on a cold winter's night reading a book crammed full of spooky tales. There is something in human nature that makes us actually enjoy being frightened. Even when the book is closed, the characters still menacingly play out their roles inside our heads, keeping us awake with one eye tiredly watching the shadows in the corner of the bedroom, just in case! Even the sceptic who dismisses the whole thing as "rubbish" has a story to tell, often announcing "but there was this one time when …"

There is always this "one time" in everybody's life when we thought we had seen a ghostly figure out of the corner of our eye, but when we swung our head round to take a look, there was nobody there! At least, nobody we could see! There is something in the human psyche that makes us prefer to listen to someone else recounting a ghostly yarn rather than experiencing it for ourselves. But that said, personal experience is far more reliable and much more intriguing than hearing anecdotal accounts that happened to someone else. I have personally been involved in thousands of paranormal cases, and have been fortunate to make detailed analyses of both haunted people as well as haunted locations. Although many cases have proven to be a waste of time, a minority have been really intriguing and left me in no doubt that the occurring phenomena were produced by a disembodied source.

I have been mediumistically inclined since I was a child; my mother, her mother, and my mother's sister were mediums, and so as a child, seeing so-called "dead" people was commonplace to me.

My life as a medium and paranormal investigator has never been dull, and no two paranormal cases are ever the same. I am now far too long in the tooth to take my career for granted, and today I see the paranormal as a sort of calling rather than a job, unlike the hundreds of paranormal groups that have suddenly appeared all over the UK and America over the last ten years or so. Although the paranormal has become an extremely fashionable business, for me personally it is like embarking upon an exciting journey into unknown terrain.

I have been a professional medium for over thirty years now and have appeared on television worldwide. As well as presenting my own thirty-six-week television series *Secrets of the Paranormal*, I also spent twelve months on the popular television series *Most Haunted*. I founded the Thought Workshop, the UK's first Centre for Psychic and Spiritual Studies and Alternative Therapies, visited by students from all over the world. Although this closed in the early 1990s, in 2001 I established the Billy Roberts Paranormal Study Centre in the famous Penny Lane (of Beatles fames) in Liverpool, England, where I ran courses and workshops on a wide range of esoteric and metaphysical subjects.

As well as my own experiences, people are always eager to contact my office to relate their own spooky tales, the majority of which have never ceased to fascinate and intrigue me. As I have already explained, even the sceptic has a spooky tale to tell. Over the years I have collected thousands of stories, and these have culminated into an ideal book with which to curl up on the settee on a cold and blustery winter's night.

Some of the spine-chilling stories included in this book are quite gruesome, and others reflect the frailties of human emotions. I have done my best to present an eclectic collection of balanced stories; including spooky tales, tongue-in-cheek stories, and stories to bring a tear to your eye and cause your heart to leap. Even the urban myths the majority of us have grown up with cannot be dismissed, as the mysterious world of the unknown is full of surprises, and tales that transcend the bounds of the imagination can occur at any time.

The spooky tales contained in this book suit every human emotion and need. Allow me to now take you into the mysterious land of the unknown. Do you think you are in the house alone while reading this book? If so, then think again. There is always somebody or something watching you from the shadows.

ONE

The Unexplained

Some things simply defy human understanding and cannot be explained no matter how hard we try. There is no end of stories of people attending their own funerals, phone calls from the dead, or ordinary individuals who find themselves confronted by the devil. Why these things happen to us mortals God alone knows, but they do. And all those tales that take us one step closer to the veil that separates this world from the next will always fascinate and intrigue us—until that day when we too reside beyond earthly shadows and are able to discover the secrets of the dead.

The Invitation

This is what transpired when a distraught woman came to me for a private consultation after her husband had died while she was out shopping. The information gleaned during the session revealed to the grieving wife exactly what happened to her husband, and as a result helped her to come to terms with her loss.

Gladys Macklin couldn't believe that her marriage to Bernard had lasted thirty years. Her mother, Joan, had doubted that it would survive twelve months, let alone thirty years. Neither of Gladys's parents had liked Bernard the first time she brought him home. "A bit rough!" said her mother. "Doesn't speak much!" commented her father. Needless to say, as Gladys had predicted, once they really got to know him, they both soon changed their minds and gradually grew to regard him as their own son. Bernard had been good to them both: he used to take Joan for a drive when she was ill, and after she died, he would take his father-in-law, Jim, to the Dog and Horse for a pint every Thursday night without fail. Gladys's father had always looked forward to his time with Bernard, which gave him the opportunity to reminisce about the good old days when his wife was alive. For that couple of hours on a Thursday night, Bernard had been a captive audience as his father-in-law delighted in telling him stories Bernard had heard so many times before. But he didn't mind; he loved Jim like his own father and always enjoyed hearing about how he had met his wife Joan at the local ballroom when she was only sixteen years old. Although it was expected, when Jim died after a short illness, Bernard was just as upset as his wife. He had not only lost a father-in-law, he had lost his drinking partner and best friend.

Although Gladys and Bernard had planned to celebrate their thirtieth wedding anniversary quietly, they were still overjoyed when their daughter, Angie, threw a surprise party for them at a local club. The music was provided by an Irish folk band, who played Gladys's and Bernard's favourite traditional Irish music that they'd first been introduced to while on holiday in Dublin.

Although Gladys had to keep an eye on her husband's drinking, the night went well with everyone enjoying themselves.

As the band put away their equipment and the night slowly came to an end, Gladys and Bernard gave their thanks and said goodbye to everyone.

"You'd better get dad home before he falls over," laughed Angie, amused by her father's face. "I've phoned for a taxi for you."

Although they both enjoyed the party, Gladys knew from experience that it would take her husband a couple of days to recover.

"It was worth it though!" he said, sipping his coffee. "We must do it again next year."

Gladys shook her head and raised her brows. "By the look of you I doubt very much that you'll be here next year. You just don't know when to stop."

"Once in a while never hurt anybody." She had heard her husband's excuses many times, and just shook her head in disbelief. Gladys was not a drinker. She knew her limitations, and although she did have a glass or two of champagne at the party, she needed to keep a clear head to keep an eye on her husband. Bernard liked his drink and would drink anything in front of him. Little wonder he had such a hangover.

Since they were both retired, they went everywhere together. Although he hated shopping, Bernard even accompanied his wife to the supermarket every Friday morning. Their daughter Angie was married with children, so they were able to get away every weekend in the summer. The mortgage had been paid and they had nothing on finance, so for Gladys and Bernard life was pretty idyllic.

"I need a few things from the supermarket," said Gladys, slipping her arm into her coat. "You'd better stay here. You look as white as a ghost."

"I couldn't go even if you wanted me to!" mumbled Bernard incoherently, gently rubbing his chest. "I've got terrible heartburn!"

"No wonder, with the amount you drank last night!" She buttoned her coat and shook her head in exasperation. "I don't know what to do with you Bernard Macklin. Anyway, I won't be long. There's some indigestion relief in the bathroom cabinet."

When his wife had gone Bernard decided to have a snooze in front of the fire. He never slept well when he had been drinking and felt so tired. "Just forty winks until Gladys gets back," he said, closing his eyes. And within moments he was fast asleep.

He had no idea how long he had been asleep. For some unknown reason the clock on the mantel had stopped, and his wife was still not back. He knew how she liked to talk and so he just assumed that Gladys had probably met someone she knew in the supermarket and had stopped for a chat. He smiled to himself when he thought of how his wife would talk to anyone. He was just about to put the kettle on to make a cup of coffee, when the doorbell went.

Two smartly dressed men stood on the doorstep, smiling. They looked like Jehovah's Witnesses to Bernard, and he was just about to close the door in their faces, when one man spoke. "We have brought you a very special invitation, Bernard." He was still very tired, and his head was still fuzzy from the night before. But Bernard wondered how they knew his name and was sufficiently intrigued to know more.

"What do you mean, a special invitation?" He pulled back the door and stepped onto the path outside.

"Your wife is already there." The other man smiled, gesturing to the plush limousine waiting outside the house. "Your car awaits you!"

"My wife never said anything to me!" Bernard said, bewildered. "She told me she was going shopping."

"It was sprung on her unexpectedly," the man said quickly. "Everybody is waiting for you." One of the men walked down the path towards the car, then opened the door, gesturing for Bernard to get in.

"You'd better get your coat!" the other man reminded him. "Your wife said to tell you to put on your nice blue jacket."

Although puzzled, Bernard did as the man suggested, and within moments he was being driven along the road in silence, destination unknown.

The car had travelled for no more than two miles when it pulled up outside of St. Michael's church, just on the edge of town.

"This is where we got married!" said Bernard nostalgically, suddenly thinking that perhaps his wife had arranged for them to renew their vows. "I should have put on my suit! Maybe there's time for me to go back and at least put on a tie."

One of the men shook his head and smiled warmly. "You can't go back now Bernard. It doesn't matter how you are dressed, this is your day and everyone is waiting for you." By now the car's door had been opened and Bernard climbed onto the pavement. As he looked up at the church spire, he was suddenly overwhelmed with panic. Noticing this, the two men took Bernard's arms before slowly leading him along the path and into the vestibule of the church. His senses were somehow heightened, and even the sound of the church organ seemed to hurt his ears. For a few moments, his eyes were blurred and he stood in the aisle disoriented, and was supported by the two men. "I had a bit too much to drink last night!" He said, shaking his head with embarrassment. It took him a few moments to collect his thoughts and focus clearly before he was able to walk into the church. He was surprised to see it nearly full, and noticed his wife sitting with his daughter and her husband at the very front near the altar. Before moving any further, Bernard had a good look to see who was there. There were many people he knew and a few he couldn't recall at all. He looked quizzically at the two men who had brought him. They had stopped smiling and were now standing there with their hands clasped in front of them, staring solemnly at Bernard. One of the men gestured for Bernard to make his way down the aisle towards the front of the church. He felt apprehensive but was also overcome with a sense of excitement. His wife was always full of surprises, he thought. Although a little annoyed that she hadn't given him enough time to get ready, he was amazed that she had managed to keep it a secret from him. Although Bernard wasn't the least bit romantic, his wife was, and had always wanted to renew their vows. In fact, his wife knew him so well, she probably knew that this would be the only way she could have gotten him into the church. There was no disputing their love for each other, and in a way Bernard felt quite pleased. For a few moments, he found himself reflecting upon his life, with the good and bad times passing quickly through his mind. He found himself thinking about his childhood, his teenage years, and how he met his wife in the first place. "Now's not the time to be nostalgic!" he reminded himself. "I've got to pull myself together."

The last thunderous sound of the organ gradually faded into silence, and all that could now be heard echoing through the church were the nervous shuffling of feet and the occasional gentle sob. Bernard wondered why his wife and daughter were crying. "Overcome with emotion," he thought, feeling somewhat touched by it all himself. He tried to go to them but his feet felt like lead weights and he could scarcely move one in front of the other on the cold floor, almost as though some powerful invisible force was stopping him. His attention was suddenly caught by the minister stepping forward. "This is it!" he thought. "It's just like getting married all over again."

"Our thoughts go out to the family of Bernard Macklin…" The minister's words echoed solemnly through the church, as he lowered his eyes to the several pieces of paper he was holding in his hands. "Particularly to his wife, Gladys, for her sad loss, and his daughter, Angie."

"What?" Bernard gasped, as panic gripped him and he realised what was happening. He wasn't there to renew his wedding vows; he was there for his own funeral. "No!"

he cried out, turning to the two men who were now silently watching him from the far end of the aisle. "No! This can't be right!" He turned to face his wife and could see the sadness on her face as she was consoled by his daughter. "I'm not dead!" he called out to her. "There has been some sort of mistake. Look at me. I'm here!" But Gladys couldn't hear him! Nobody could hear or see him now.

Within no time at all, the service had reached its conclusion, and as Bernard watched his coffin being carried slowly from the church, he felt as though he was being sucked in to a huge vacuum, as everything receded into nothingness.

The Wrong Number

Brenda Gibson had lived in her quaint terrace house for five years and had decided that it was now time to make a few changes to her life. The year was coming to an end and she was determined that 1959 would be her year with a new beginning. She had been divorced for two years and although her husband, Ron, still called to see the children and had frequently intimated that he would very much like to get involved with her again, she had no plans of ever returning to him.

"Never go back!" her mother had always advised her as a general matter of principle. "Always move forward."

And that was exactly what Brenda intended to do.

She had been to the estate agents to find out what sort of prices the houses were fetching in the area and had immediately taken the decision to sell up and move perhaps to a country village, where she had always wanted to live. Now that she was in a much better financial situation, she just knew that the time was right for her to make a new start.

On the Friday afternoon, after the children had gone back to school, Brenda decided to catch the bus into town to treat herself to a new coat and shoes. She was just about to leave the house when the telephone rang. The caller asked to speak to someone called Jean, and when she told him that he must have the wrong number, he became abusive and then hung up.

Although the call had unnerved Brenda somewhat, she quickly put it from her mind and made her way towards High Street to catch the bus to go shopping in town. On her return, she had just put the key in the lock when she heard the telephone ringing again. She deposited her shopping on the floor in the hallway and quickly rushed to answer it.

"Where have you been?" demanded the voice at the other end of the line. "I've been trying to get you all afternoon."

It was the same man who had been abusive earlier, and Brenda felt a rush of fear, which caused her heart to beat faster.

"Who is this?" she snapped, desperately trying her best not to appear afraid. "I have told you, no one called Jean lives here. If you ring again, I'll have to call the police."

The man became abusive once more and even addressed her by name. He also appeared to know that she was divorced and that she lived alone with her two daughters. Brenda quickly hung up on him. She could feel herself shaking and her heart racing and did not know what to do next. As she stood by the telephone, trying to decide whether or not to call the police, it began to ring again. She allowed it to keep on ringing for some time without answering it, but the persistent noise eventually prompted her to pick up the receiver. At first she did not speak and simply listened. She could hear someone breathing at the other end of the line and some of her fear was replaced by a sudden rush of anger.

"I've just phoned the police!" she shouted down the phone, half expecting him to hang up.

"No you haven't!" he coolly replied, with an arrogant, sneering tone. "You haven't phoned anyone. You'd better take care, living alone with your two lovely daughters."

"You're a pervert!" she screamed, slamming down the phone.

The telephone calls had left her emotionally drained and she decided almost immediately to carry out her threat and call the police.

It took the police some time to respond, but eventually a policewoman called at the house the following afternoon.

Although she took down all the details of the anonymous calls, Brenda noticed that she seemed completely uninterested in the incidents and was only half listening to what she was saying. So she expressed her concern and stressed that she desperately wanted something to be done about it.

The abusive telephone calls came every day at approximately the same time and, on each occasion, Brenda reported them to the police without any satisfaction. Eventually, she called the local police station to lodge a formal complaint. She filled in a statement there and then and was assured that something would be done. However, she had no sooner returned home, than the duty sergeant at the police station rang her.

"We are putting a trace on all your calls," he assured her. "There's no guarantee that we'll catch the caller, but at least it might deter him."

Satisfied that the police were now going to do something about the problem, Brenda breathed a sigh of relief and sat down with a nice cup of tea and a digestive biscuit, feeling much more relaxed than she had since the calls had begun.

But, no sooner had she settled down on the settee, than the anonymous menace telephoned again.

"You shouldn't have gone to the police," he hissed, threateningly. "You're a naughty girl, and naughty girls get punished."

Brenda knew that she had to keep him talking so that the police would have enough time to trace the number he was calling from.

"How do you know I've been to the police?" she asked, her voice shaking nervously. "Or are you surmising?"

"I know everything about you," he continued. "You're also thinking about moving house."

Brenda froze. She hadn't even told her daughters about her intention to move house and wondered how on earth he could know so many details about her life.

"I don't know what you're talking about," she bluffed. "I wouldn't dream of leaving here. I love it."

"You're right!" he hissed. "You won't be going anywhere."

He began to sound even more threateningly aggressive, almost manic.

"I'm going to pay you and your daughters a visit soon!"

At that point the line went dead. No more than thirty minutes later, two policemen called to see Brenda.

"Did you manage to trace the number?" she asked eagerly. "Have you caught him?"

They followed her into the living room and suggested that she sit down. They looked quite serious and were glancing nervously at each other.

"How long have you lived here, Mrs. Gibson?" asked one of the policemen.

"Why?" she asked, curiously, her eyes moving from one to the other. "What's that got to do with the phone calls?"

"How long, Mrs. Gibson?" the policeman insisted, a note of urgency in his voice.

"Approximately five years," she answered. "But why?"

The policeman who was speaking looked at his colleague with a somewhat puzzled expression on his face. The other police officer then continued to explain.

"I really don't know how to tell you this." He paused, and then glanced uncomfortably at his colleague. "This may sound quite strange, but you see, we traced the number to this address." He watched Brenda for a response. "In fact, it was traced to your own number."

"What?" she retorted. "It's not possible. I've only got one phone."

"We know," confirmed the policeman. "We checked our records and Alan McCarthy lived here fifteen years ago. He was cautioned several times by the police for making obscene phone calls to a middle-aged lady on the other side of town." He paused, and lowered his eyes uncomfortably. "In fact, he murdered her."

"Oh, my God!" Brenda gasped. "And he's obviously out of prison now and planning to do the same to me. I hope you're going to arrest him before he does any harm to me or my children?"

The two policemen looked at each other, and then turned to face her. There was a moment's silence before one of them spoke.

"That won't be possible, Mrs. Gibson," he said solemnly. "You see, Alan McCarthy is dead! He committed suicide shortly after he murdered the woman in her home."

"I don't understand!" Brenda stuttered. "But how ..."

"We don't understand it either, Mrs. Gibson," the policeman interrupted, who was now smiling. "But at least you can be sure of one thing, Alan McCarthy's not in any position to do you or your family any harm."

Brenda glanced at the policeman, still with a concerned look on her face.

"Are you absolutely sure about that?" she said brusquely. "Because I'm not!"

The ghostly telephone calls did continue right up until Brenda Gibson moved to another house. The people who bought the house from her also received the same mysterious phone calls for a period of about six months. Then, for some unknown reason, they stopped completely. Maybe Alan McCarthy had no means of paying his phone bill and was cut off!

The Devil Calls

"Never play cards on a Sunday," my grandmother always warned. "The devil will get you!" In 1768, Jack Clegg did just that. In fact, he always looked forward to his friends calling on him on a Friday night to drink ale and play cards. They would stay in his cottage until the sun came up and all the ale had been drunk. Jack Clegg's wife had left him because of his gambling and drunken ways and now, although he was in his mid-fifties, he lived the life of a single man and was very rarely sober.

On an extremely cold Sunday night two weeks before Christmas, there had been a snowstorm all over the Northwest of England. Jack Clegg had backed up the fire with logs and stocked his larder with ale and eagerly awaited his friends, Joe Mathews and Tom Tilsley, who were due to arrive at around nine p.m. As it was Jack's birthday, they had decided to do some additional serious drinking on the Sunday as well as the customary Friday. Tom and Joe were both married with families, and so to be allowed out again on the Sunday, they had to come up with some good excuses. Jack Clegg was not a well-liked man; Tom and Joe were his only friends and had been since they were children together. Jack frequently became aggressive with drink but Tom and Joe knew exactly how to handle him.

"Bring plenty of money with you," Jack had warned. "I'm feeling lucky."

The three friends settled down to their bonus night of drinking, merriment, and cards. It had been snowing all day long and the log fire roared up the chimney as Jack poured the ale and Joe dealt the cards. By the time the clock on the mantelpiece struck midnight, the three of them were quite drunk. Tom had won most of the games and Jack was quite angry.

Joe quickly defused the situation by reassuring Jack that he would win it all back before the night was out.

Jack was in the middle of pouring each man another pot of ale, when there was a knock on the door.

Wondering who it could be at that time of night, he staggered drunkenly to his feet and reluctantly made his way to the door.

"If it's my Beth," sniggered Tom, "tell her I'm not here."

They chuckled as Jack pulled back the door. On the step, shivering in the cold, was a young man wearing a black cape and a top hat. He was blue with the cold and asked Jack if he could shelter for an hour from the snow-storm.

Thinking it was an ideal opportunity to entice the young man into playing cards and take his money, Jack cordially invited him in from the cold. The stranger looked well-to-do and that, to Jack, meant he had money. "I hope you're a drinking man?"

The young man nodded and moved immediately towards the fire to warm his hands.

"What are you doing out on such a night?" asked Joe. "The devil himself wouldn't venture out on a night like this."

The young man smiled as he removed his cape and hung it carefully on the back of the door, before explaining that he had gone to meet a friend, but he hadn't shown up.

"No wonder!" interjected Tom. "The weather's awful and it's bound to get worse, I can feel it in my bones. You've come to the right place anyway, lad. We've got plenty of ale and money to lose."

Jack gestured for the young man to pull up his chair closer to the table.

"I hope you've got plenty of money with you?"

The young man nodded politely and retrieved a leather pouch from the pocket of his waistcoat, which was bulging with coins. He ostentatiously pulled the pouch open and emptied a pile of gold coins onto the table. Jack and his friends looked at each other in disbelief, their eyes wide with the prospect of winning it all.

Happy now that there was serious money to be won, Jack Clegg remarked that they usually only played for small stakes. Then Jack eagerly poured the young man a pot of ale.

"I hope you're not a professional gambler?" Tom joked. "We're just simple folk who enjoy the social activity of a game or two of cards." He looked sideways at his friends and winked mischievously.

Jack invited the stranger to deal the first hand and the three men watched intently as he dealt the cards clumsily onto the table like an amateur. But he went on to anger Jack by winning the first two games.

Putting it down to beginner's luck, Jack was certain the young man would not win another game.

But the stranger remained quite calm and was not going to be intimidated which infuriated Jack even more. In fact, the young stranger kept on winning until Jack's money had all gone.

The stranger declined to take Jack Clegg's IOU, which he had scribbled on a faded piece of parchment.

"You have no money," grinned the stranger. "What good is your IOU to me?"

Jack slammed his fist onto the table, angrily protesting that the stranger had taken all his money, and demanding to be given the chance to win it back.

The young stranger sat back on his chair and grinned at Jack across the table. "I repeat," he said coldly. "You have no money."

Jack's face was red with rage but his friends restrained him, assuring him that they would win all his money back for him.

Tom shuffled the cards and dealt the next game, accidentally dropping a card onto the floor. He stooped to retrieve it from beneath the table and was horrified to discover that the young man had cloven hooves instead of feet. He leapt up, banging his head carelessly on the table in his haste, and then made a dash for the door, leaving jack and Joe sitting there completely bewildered.

"It's the devil!" Tom shrieked, as he tried desperately to pull the door open. But for some reason it would not budge.

The young stranger grinned sardonically, his grin slowly turning into evil laughter. Tom's friends immediately went to help him open the door and, with a great deal of effort, it swung open. But they were horrified to see that the cottage had somehow sunk into the ground and the doorway was blocked with earth, preventing their escape. Petrified, they turned to look at the young stranger, who by now had metamorphosed into the most horrific devil-like form that he really was, snarling and laughing hideously at their fear. His insane laughter echoed around the walls of the small cottage and he screamed out the most horrible, blood-curdling cries that they had ever heard. "You are mine!" he crackled. "I have won your souls."

For some reason, which shall never really be known, the devil allowed Joe Mathews to escape, to tell the tale perhaps. However, he apparently died four weeks later from some unknown malady. The roof of the house was discovered when the snowstorms had passed, and Jack Clegg's cottage was excavated. To everyone's horror, Jack Clegg and Tom Tilsley were discovered sitting rigidly, bolt-upright, on their chairs at the table, both stone dead, and each with a look of frozen horror on their faces. No trace of anyone else was found in the cottage, and so Joe Mathews's story could not be confirmed, and was simply dismissed as the rambling words of a madman. Joe Mathews was in fact a direct descendent of my father's family.

A church was later built on the very site of Jack Clegg's cottage, and today luxury apartments mark the spot. Unexplainable paranormal phenomena in the apartments has been frequently reported, such as wailing voices in the dead of night and numerous playing cards scattered across the rooms. Perhaps they're the devil's calling cards!

The Man Who Went to His Own Funeral

Joe Francis's death came as no surprise to anyone who had known him. He smoked eighty cigarettes a day, and the amount of alcohol he consumed in a week had greatly increased over the past few years. "It's my only enjoyment!" he had always said. "Besides, you've got to die of something, haven't you?"

Although Joe had a family, his wife had left him for another man some years ago, and he had very little contact with his two daughters. He lived in a one-bedroom apartment in the town, a stone's throw from his favourite pub. Joe's oldest friend had always joked that it was the drink that kept him alive. This was, in fact, closer to the truth than anyone realised.

One fateful day Joe Francis was found dead in his apartment, apparently of a massive heart attack. Apart from Joe's friend Alf Swain and his wife, and Joe's two daughters and their husbands, no one else attended the funeral.

Alf Swain had grown up with Joe and had gone to the same school. They had both joined the army together and had fought in France during the Second World War. In their younger years, the two friends had been inseparable, and although Alf knew that Joe was now better off, he also knew he would miss his old drinking mate. Alf felt so sad, but more for himself than for Joe.

It was a cold blustery day and Alf and his wife, Peggy, sat at the back of the chapel watching as Joe's coffin was carried in. Alf leaned over to whisper something to her, when he realised someone had sat down in front of them. Alf raised his brows and gave his wife a curious glance. They had both thought it very strange that the man had sat so close to them when the tiny chapel was nearly empty. Alf knew all of Joe's drinking cronies, and wondered who the man was. He looked in his mid-thirties and was smartly dressed, but both Alf and Peggy thought it very strange that the man never moved at all during the service—he just sat staring blankly towards the front of the chapel. He didn't even bother to stand when the minister requested.

It wasn't until the service was over and everyone had got up to leave that the stranger turned to face Alf and Peggy. He was smiling knowingly at them, and then said in a low voice: "See ya, Alf!" Then he left the chapel without saying another word. Peggy could see that her husband's face was pale and for a few moments he was unable to speak.

"Are you alright, Alf?" she asked, placing a concerned hand on his arm. "Sit down for a moment."

"No, I'm okay," he said, the colour suddenly returning to his cheeks and he smiled. "You'll never guess who
that was? I just can't believe it!"

"Who?" she answered quizzically. "One of Joe's family
I would have thought. He did have a look of Joe."

"That was Joe!" He grinned. "That was Joe when he
was a young man."

"Don't be stupid!" she said, thinking that her husband
was suffering from delayed shock. "Joe's dead! Don't you
remember, that's why we're here? Let's get you home."

"It was Joe, I'm telling you," he insisted, as Peggy gently hurried him from the chapel. She stopped to retrieve
something from where the stranger had been sitting.

"What's this?" she muttered, holding it to her face for
closer inspection. It was an old photograph of two young
soldiers sitting outside a French café drinking beer. Peggy's mouth suddenly fell open when she realised who the
soldiers actually were. "This is you!" she announced. "You
and …" She stopped.

"Me and Joe." Alf grinned "This is me and my mate
Joe. He must've come to say goodbye."

Stop the Clocks

Jim Becket was a retired builder and spent most of his spare
time indulging himself in his favourite hobby either making or fixing clocks. Ever since he was a child, he'd always
had a fascination with clocks, and to his wife's dismay, the

house was full of clocks of all different types and sizes, relentlessly ticking the minutes away and chiming tumultuously together on the hour.

Jim's parents had expected him to pursue his interest as a career, but unfortunately one thing led to another and he found himself following his father's footsteps into the building trade instead. However, this did not stop him still collecting old clocks. In fact, walking into his workshop in the small room at the back of the house was just like walking into a clockmaker's shop.

The workshop's walls were strategically lined with many different kinds of clocks, modern and antique—everything from large pendulum clocks to the smallest intricate time pieces. Row upon row of clocks could be seen, ticking and chiming and driving Jim's wife, Molly, almost out of her mind. There was absolutely nothing that Jim Becket did not know about clocks, and with a steady hand and a keen eye, he could fix almost any make or style, regardless of size or intricacy of mechanism.

It was Thursday afternoon and Molly had been to the nearby shops. Overladen with bags of groceries, she struggled to put the key in the lock, cursing her husband in a low voice for not hearing her coming and opening the door for her. Eventually she managed to push the door back and placed her shopping bags on the hallway floor whilst she extricated the key from the lock.

A deadly hush suddenly overcame Molly and she paused for a moment to listen. She checked her watch; it was exactly four o'clock and yet she could not hear any of the usual chimes from her husband's huge and noisy collection of clocks.

She knew instinctively that something was not quite right and, leaving her shopping where it was, she dashed quickly into the back room, anxiously calling her husband's name. Before Molly had even got as far as the back room door, she saw him lying in a heap on the floor. She bent over to help him, but soon realised that he was dead. His purple face and still and lifeless body caused Molly to shake uncontrollably and she sobbed.

A postmortem revealed that Jim Becket had died from a massive heart attack. All Jim's clocks had stopped exactly on the hour of three o'clock—the coroner's estimated time of his death.

Although Jim Becket's clocks never worked properly again after his death, his favourite, wall-mounted clock still chimes even today, for some strange reason, regularly every 29th October—Jim's birthday.

The Crystal Ball

When Julie Watson and her husband, Joey, wandered into the old junk shop at the edge of town, they had no idea that their purchase would cause so much distress. They both shared a mutual interest in antiques, and Joey had a particular interest in pre-war toys, and it was their respective hobbies that led the couple into Fred Wilson's Antique Emporium. As soon as Julie clapped eyes on the old and very scratched crystal ball standing amongst other junk on the cluttered shelf, she immediately decided that she must have it. She held it carefully in her hands, peering wide-eyed into its distorted surface. "Do you think they can really see anything in crystal balls?" she asked, holding it in front of her husband.

"No, it's a load of rubbish," he quickly dismissed. Moving his eyes back to the old toys he was nostalgically inspecting in his hands. He added, "Don't know what you want that for anyway. What will you do with it?"

Julie's mind was made up. She had already decided to buy the crystal ball and couldn't wait to find out if she could see anything in it. Her husband just shook his head impatiently and rolled his eyes heavenward as she handed the crystal ball to the elderly bald man who had been watching her intently from behind the counter, "I'll take it!" she said, with a look of achievement on her face.

"That'll be two pounds," said the man eagerly, wrapping it in a used piece of tissue paper. "Sorry I haven't got a bag."

"That's okay," Julie answered politely. "The car's just outside."

Long before they had arrived back home, Julie had already decided that the crystal ball would make a nice ornamental feature in the cabinet she had inherited from her grandmother.

Like her mother, Julie had always been superstitious. She polished the crystal ball until it almost looked alive, before placing it proudly in her grandmother's cabinet along with other inherited pieces. She was amazed just how well the crystal ball had cleaned up, and even remarked to her husband that the scratches were no longer apparent.

Two weeks had gone by and Julie was giving the front room a last-minute cleaning before her husband arrived home from work. It was Friday and she had taken the kids to stay with her mother for the weekend. "A nice peaceful weekend with just the two of us." She sighed as she pushed the vacuum cleaner quickly across the carpet. The late-afternoon sun filtered through the lace curtains throwing fragmented shards of light off the crystal ball standing in the cabinet. Julie stopped for a moment mesmerised by the eye-catching display, and as the sunlight suddenly dipped behind a cloud, a shadow obscured the crystal ball for a few moments, before lighting it up again. That's when she thought she could see images flashing quickly across the surface of the crystal ball, one after another, as clear as a TV picture. Unknown faces and landscapes appeared in the crystal ball as quickly as flicking through the pages of a picture book. Enthralled, Julie moved closer to the cabinet and was amazed to see the grotesque face of a man peering out at her, malevolence in his dark, deep-set eyes.

She quickly unlocked the cabinet, pulled back the door fully, and carefully retrieved the crystal ball. She held it gently in her hands and watched the man's face as it slowly metamorphosed into the face of someone both she and her husband knew well. "My god!" she gasped. "Peter Ridley. What the..." She stopped as the face of one of her husband's oldest friends slowly changed again, this time into a woman's face she did not know.

The woman's faced grimaced as though she was in great pain, and then the crystal ball looked as though blood had been splashed all over it. Julie was so horrified that she dropped the crystal ball onto the floor and watched wide-eyed as it rolled across the carpet, its momentum ceasing as it reached the edge of the settee. Stooping to retrieve it, she noticed that the images were no longer visible and the well-polished surface of the crystal ball just glistened in the light and the reflection of Julie's own face was all that could be seen...She thought no more about it, and only mentioned it to her husband after he said he had met Peter Ridley on his way home from work.

"It was most probably a trick of the light." Her husband shook his head dismissively. "You know what you're like." However, after they had finished their evening meal, Joey told his wife that a girlfriend of Peter's had been murdered some years ago, and although the police had brought his friend in for routine questioning, his watertight alibi made it clear that he had nothing whatsoever to do with it.

"Besides," said Joey, shaking the creases from the evening newspaper, "he couldn't harm a fly and all his friends know that only too well." Nonetheless, Julie had a very suspicious mind, and she knew only too well that what she had seen was very real.

Over a week had passed by, and Julie's daughters Samantha and Kim were watching TV in the living room whilst she caught up on some paperwork in the front room where it was quiet. She despised doing her monthly accounts and allowed her thoughts to drift away for a moment from the laborious chore of making ends meet. Her attention was suddenly caught by a piercing bright light on the crystal ball's surface in the cabinet, and as she moved closer, she saw the same grotesque face staring out and grinning menacingly at her. As before she saw the face change into the face of her husband's friend, Peter Ridley. She took a step back as she saw another face appear across the surface of the crystal ball. It was the face of a young black woman with a look of sheer terror in her eyes. Again, it seemed to Julie as though the young woman was pleading to her for help. Julie's heart began to pound inside her chest, and she watched helplessly as the crystal ball fell into darkness. All that she could now see was the reflection of her own face on the shiny surface of the crystal ball.

Julie didn't really know what to think. Being the sceptic he was, she knew her husband would laugh at her. However, the following evening she couldn't believe the front-page headlines in the local newspaper: "Twenty-two-year-old prostitute found dead in alleyway." Underneath that was a picture of the young black girl she had seen reflected in the crystal ball.

Julie's husband could see that his wife was perturbed "What's the matter with you?" he asked, concerned. "You look as though you have seen a ghost!"

"I think I have!" she said quietly, allowing the newspaper to fall to her lap. "In fact, I know I have."

She told her husband everything she had seen, before lifting the newspaper to show him the headlines. Joey was concerned about his wife's obvious distress and could see no alternative but to get rid of the crystal ball. Without saying another word Joey lifted the crystal ball from the cabinet and, before Julie could say anything, he had disappeared through the door.

He'd been gone nearly an hour when he returned with a look of achievement all over his face. "That's the end of that!"

"What have you done with it?" Julie asked. "I hope you haven't given it to someone?"

Joey shook his head and grinned. "I took it down to the river." He sat back triumphantly. "No one will ever see that thing ever again, that's for sure."

A few days later they saw the astounding news on the front pages of the evening newspaper; Peter Ridley had been arrested for the murder of a young prostitute.

"They've apparently got a lot of evidence against him," Joey said solemnly shaking his head. "It's a cut and dried case. And it looks like the police are going to charge him with three other murders. I just can't believe it."

Julie felt an icy chill run down her spine as she recalled the images she had seen in the crystal ball, and was so glad her husband had got rid of it.

Against Julie's better judgment, some weeks later the couple called into the junk shop to see if there was anything of interest they could buy. "No crystal balls or Ouija boards," Joey joked, giving his wife a warning sideways glance. "Be warned!"

Now there was a middle-aged woman sitting behind the counter, reading a magazine. When Julie and Joey walked into the shop, she peered over her wire-rimmed spectacles at them and smiled. "Looking for anything in particular?" she asked politely. "Or have you just come to browse?"

"Just come to browse," answered Julie, following her husband to the far end of the shop. Almost at the same time they stopped in disbelief, wide-eyed, as they both saw the old crystal ball sitting on the shelf amongst other miscellaneous pieces. Joey reached out and collected the crystal sphere from the shelf. "It couldn't be the same one," he exclaimed, almost breathlessly. "I threw it in the river." He grinned dismissively before returning the crystal ball to the shelf. "Obviously another one."

Not convinced, Julie quickly took the crystal ball in her hands and began to examine it closely. "No!" she said, "It's the same one. I'd know it anywhere." She pointed to a deep scratch across the smooth surface. "Look!" she urged her husband to take a closer look. "The scratch has a little loop at the end of it. This is the same one."

"Ridiculous!" her husband said with a grin, turning to make his way to the other side of the shop. "I know what I did with it."

Listening to the couple discussing the crystal ball, the shopkeeper removed her spectacles and placed them carefully alongside the magazine she had been reading on top of the cluttered counter. "Is there something wrong?" she asked, pulling herself tiredly to her feet. She made her way over to where Julie was standing holding the old crystal ball. "It's a very old crystal ball, with a lot of history."

Julie looked at the woman in almost disbelief. "We bought one just like it from here some weeks ago." She watched the woman's face for a response. "An elderly man served us."

The woman smiled. "I'm the only one who works here," she said. "I've owned the business for over fifteen years, and before that my father owned it."

Julie swung round to face her husband, before looking at the woman once again. "Maybe you were not in the shop that day? Maybe your father was in the shop?"

"If only that were the case," said the woman, a far-away look in her eyes. "My father died over ten years ago now. He was an unusual man." She took the crystal ball from Julie and began turning it slowly in her hands, her thoughts drifting nostalgically back through the years. "This was my father's crystal ball, and his father's before him. It's not for sale and never has been. It's been on the shelf since the day he died. I always feel as though he is watching me from somewhere in the crystal ball. And this gives me great comfort."

Julie glanced at her husband and smiled. They both now realised why she was meant to have owned the crystal ball in the first place, albeit for a short time.

The Lady Who Fought the Devil

Teresa Helena Higginson was born in Holywell, North Wales, UK, in 1844, and from a very early age it was clear to her parents that she was a very unusual child. She was quite small for her age and clearly in poor health. In 1854, at the age of ten, Teresa was sent with her two sisters to be educated at the Convent of Mercy in Nottingham, UK, where she stayed until she was twenty-one. She then returned to where her parents were then living in St. Helens, Merseyside, the UK. By now she had become very religious and devoted much of her spare time to prayer and meditation. Teresa's poor health meant that she spent much of her time at home in bed, where her sisters took turns nursing her.

Her father's business encountered financial difficulties and he was forced into bankruptcy. This necessitated a change of address, and for a while the family moved from one place to another. To help her parents, Teresa Helena used her sewing skills to make extra money, and when circumstances began to improve, she trained to be a teacher. With her pleasant disposition, she was well liked by all the children, which caused her to be in great demand as a teacher. She eventually took lodgings with her closest friend, Susan Rowland, also a teacher, in one of the poorer areas of Liverpool. It was here that Teresa confided in her friend that the "devil" frequently attacked her. She also claimed that she was frequently visited by angels as well as the Virgin Mary. Her friend, Susan, frequently witnessed Teresa falling into a trance and speaking in a strange voice that was obviously not her own. Susan eventually persuaded her friend to consult a priest by the name of Father Powell. He became immediately concerned for Teresa's psychological well-being and thought that perhaps she was insane. However, after spending some time with Teresa, he witnessed her writing in a hand that was obviously not her own, causing him to quickly discard the notion that she was mad and instead became her spiritual confidant and adviser. Accompanied by Father Powell, Teresa would sit up until late writing copious pages filled with prophetic writings about future events. She predicted that huge steel ships would sail under the waters, and large crafts would fly in the air. She also predicted the two World Wars to come, and even said that Britain and Germany would be enemies but that Britain would be victorious. Teresa Helena began to suffer the wounds of the crucifixion and would frequently fall into a swoon whilst furniture was thrown about the room by some aggressive invisible force. The horrific manifestations brought terror to Teresa and her friend, but Father Powell remained faithfully by her side through all the turmoil. Even though the priest made every effort to "cast out" the demonic force, the phenomena still persisted.

News began to circulate that the devil frequently called for Teresa Helena Higginson, who bravely fought his attacks often to the detriment of her own poor health. She was eventually forced out of her lodgings, and malicious rumours began to circulate that the diminutive Teresa Helena Higginson was not the spiritual person she appeared to be, but in fact was a drunk who was frequently seen returning home late at night, falling about in the gutter in a drunken stupor. This, of course, was absurd. Teresa Helena did not touch alcohol at all, and the malicious gossip was just a prime example of how cruel and jealous people can be. Remembering the biblical precept, *"A prophet is without honour in his own village,"* Teresa accepted a teaching post some distance from her home town. News of Teresa's powers spread far and wide, and she was eventually granted an audience with Pope Pius X, who was believed to have remarked that she was a "special child of God."

Teresa Helena's encounters with the devil and angels persisted right up to the day she died. In 1905 at the age of sixty-one, whilst preparing to return to her parents' home in Neston, Merseyside, UK, for Christmas, she suffered a stroke and died. Her sisters brought her body back to the little village of Neston and she was buried in St. Winefride's Churchyard in Little Neston. Today her grave is visited by pilgrims from all over the world, who adorn it with all sorts of religious artefacts, such as rosary beads, pictures of the Virgin Mary and flowers. Steps are now being taken to bring about Teresa Helena Higginson's beatification who has now become known as the "Contemplative Saint."

In my opinion, Teresa Helena Higginson is a prime example of how a devoutly religious person, who devoted her life to God and prayer, can be targeted by demonic forces, seeking to bring about her downfall, or at worst, her demise. This is also an example of how evil can infiltrate the minds of people, causing them to decry and accuse an ordinary individual whose only desire is to serve God. It is quite clear when one looks at Teresa Helena's life, that she was also most definitely looked upon by angelic forces, and with their help and support she eventually overcame the relentless malevolent attacks. Teresa Helena Higginson most definitely lived her life with both angels and demons.

A Message from the Past

Will McPherson had been unemployed for five years, and at the age of fifty-eight had now given up all hope of getting a job. He'd become quite accustomed to his wife Barbara's accusations that he was bone idle and didn't want to work. And according to her two daughters, she was right. He spent most of his time either in his local pub drinking with friends or out metal detecting with his oldest and dearest friend, Glyn Hughes. As far as Will was concerned, he had no reason to work. The Victorian semi had been left to them by Barbara's parents, and so they had no mortgage to worry about. Barbara had a part-time job in a local supermarket, and his unemployment benefit paid for his drink. Will's almost fanatical passion for metal detecting began at a very early age, as he became fascinated with anything to do with the past. To his wife's dismay, he would spend most of his spare time either on a farm somewhere, or metal detecting on one of many Victorian rubbish tips (landfills) on the outskirts of town. Apart from numerous Roman coins, an occasional Saxon sword, and an Elizabethan cross, Will had unearthed nothing of any great value. However, he was certain that one day his luck would change and he would discover an ancient hoard of diamonds and gold. This was his dream, but in reality he knew that that's all it was—a dream! Nonetheless, Will McPherson loved those few hours spent with his friend, digging around in the soil, always believing he was a few feet away from an incredible discovery.

One Sunday morning on 3rd September 1993, as the weather didn't look to promising, Will and Glyn decided that a local dig would be preferable. At least, that way if it rained they could pop into the Dog and Gun for a few pints before making their way home. Although they had never found anything there before, they settled for a well-known Victorian tip not far from where they both lived.

It was just after ten thirty a.m., and apart from the odd jogger and a man walking his dog, everything was quiet. Over the years they'd found various small items of interest, ranging from a bent Victoria spoon to a pewter mug, as well as a never-ending collection of old, clay pipes. Any find was a great discovery to Will and Glyn, whose motto was "It's not the finding as much as it is the looking."

Only half an hour had gone by when Will got a strong response from his metal detector. After establishing the exact spot that was producing the signal, he began digging with his trowel. He had dug down no more than a foot when he made contact with a solid object. Calling out excitedly to his friend and, without pausing for breath, he continued to prise his find free from the ground. It was some sort of metal casket with a name engraved across the lid: "Charles Langton Yates."

"That's odd!" muttered Will. "That was the name of a Victorian magician and mystic who once lived in my house at the beginning of the twentieth century. He was apparently quite brilliant and performed feats that astounded his peers."

"Open it!" said Glyn eagerly. "This may well be the find we've been waiting for."

"No such luck!" replied Will sceptically. "It's probably empty, knowing my luck."

Glyn watched patiently as Will forced the lid of the box open with the edge of his trowel before reaching inside to retrieve its contents.

"What is it?" asked Glyn, as he impatiently watched Will's mucky fingers clumsily opening a piece of faded parchment. The writing on it was now quite faint and Will struggled to read it out loud to his friend, scarcely able to believe his eyes.

"To Will McPherson, who will most probably stumble across this casket. If he does, I will have achieved the impossible! I return the enclosed for your safekeeping and sincerely hope you will forgive me for any inconvenience I may have caused you. April 4th 1901. Charles Langton Yates."

"How is that possible?" gasped Glyn, with a puzzled look on his face.

Will was speechless and his hand trembled as he retrieved a leather pouch from the box and emptied its contents into the palm of his hand. Feeling increasingly bewildered and confused, he examined the contents of the pouch: a gold signet ring and an eternity ring. His face turned pale as he recognised the rings.

"What is it, Will?" prompting his friend, concerned. "Are you alright? You look as though you've seen a ghost."

"I have!" Will mumbled, as if in a trance. "These rings went missing from my house over five years ago, just after I lost my job. They disappeared completely without trace. At the time, Barbara and I were going through a bad time, and she accused me of selling them."

"But how can they be the same rings?" said Glyn incredulously. "This box has been buried for over ninety years."

"I'd know them anywhere," Will answered nostalgically. "The signet ring was my father's and I had it engraved with my initials. Look." And he offered the rings to his friend for examination. "And the eternity ring belonged to Barbara's mother."

"Good grief! You're right!" gasped Glyn, confirming the inscription on the signet ring. "WM. How is it possible?"

"The only person who can answer that is Charles Langton Yates," Will concluded. "And he is dead! Or is he?"

To Where the Narrow Road Forks

When John and Pat Rafferty first viewed the Victorian house in the suburbs of Liverpool, England, they fell in love with it immediately. John's new job with a huge electronics firm had necessitated the move from Manchester to Liverpool.

They were presently staying with Pat's parents until they had found somewhere permanent. With two children already and another one on the way, they needed a bigger house than the one they had sold in Manchester and they both agreed that the Victorian house in a quiet area of Liverpool was perfect for their expanding family. It was 1955 and Liverpool had not fully recovered from the devastation of World War II, and John was so grateful to have a good job. He had been promoted to a new position, which meant more money and far better prospects. Their baby was due in three months time, on the 15th September, so it was extremely important that they found a house quickly.

Once the mortgage had been secured, they bought the house they had both set their hearts on and moved in within six weeks. Although the decor was not to their liking, the house itself was exactly what they had both wanted. The area was quite respectable and the large rear garden made it ideal for the children.

The whole family settled down very quickly in their new home and Pat gave birth to a little girl on the 14th September, making their family complete.

When John came in from work one cold November night, he announced to Pat that he had to go to a farewell dinner for a work colleague, who was retiring at the end of the year.

"It's on the eighteenth of December," he told her. "It's being held at a hotel in Ormskirk. We haven't had a night out for ages."

Pat refused to leave the newly born baby with anybody, not even her parents, and so declined the opportunity to have a night out with her husband.

Although disappointed, Pat insisted that her husband should go and enjoy himself.

"I was hoping that you would drive," he admitted, "then I could enjoy a few drinks."

The 18th December was a cold and frosty day with a threat of thick fog in the evening, according to the weather forecast. Although the hotel was not all that far away, it was in a more rural area of Merseyside, and John was not looking forward to driving in such hazardous conditions, especially by himself. Although it was foggy by four p.m., it was not as bad as the weatherman had predicted and John had come home early from work so that he could take his time driving to the hotel. He was not really familiar with the route, so he wanted to leave in good time, just in case the weather got worse.

It took him over an hour and a half to reach Ormskirk, and he still needed to get to the hotel. By this time the fog was extremely thick and he could scarcely see the bonnet of the car, let alone the road in front of him. The headlights cast a feeble beam and only sufficed to reveal the thick, impenetrable grey fog all around him. He drove with his face as close to the windscreen as possible and had reduced his speed to 10 miles an hour. The concentration required made him feel hot and flustered and he undid his tie with a sigh of relief.

It was impossible to see any road signs or landmarks and he did not have a clue where he was, or even if he was still actually driving on the road. Pat's last words kept passing annoyingly through his mind. "Only a fool would go out on a night like this." She had warned him and he had to admit that, as always, she was right. He was a fool and now he regretted not having made some excuse not to go. After all, he hardly knew Ted Payne and had only spoken to him on three occasions in all the time they had worked together.

Stopping the car at what he had estimated was the roadside, John got out to get his bearings and to see if anyone passing by could tell him where exactly he was.

Not surprisingly, there was absolutely no one around on such an abysmal night, but he had an idea that hat he had somehow driven straight through Ormskirk and was in the middle of the countryside. He thought he could hear cows some yards away and there was the familiar damp odour of farmland in winter, intermingled with the smell of fog.

By now, John had resigned himself to the obvious fact that he was not going to make it to the function and he just wanted to be back home with his wife and children, in front of the warm fire or, better still, tucked up in bed. Instead he was stuck in thick fog, in the middle of nowhere with no clue about his exact position. He decided to drive a little further on and, if necessary, he would sleep in the car until the fog had lifted or even, perhaps, stay the night at a country inn, if he was fortunate enough to come across one.

He had driven for no more than five minutes when he reached a spot where the fog appeared to be a little thinner. He could just about distinguish the narrow road he was driving along and noticed that he had reached a fork. Pausing for a moment, John decided almost immediately to take the right fork in the road and somehow had a strange feeling that he knew exactly where he was going, as though he had been there before, even though he knew this was not the case.

Eventually he found himself parked at the gates of what looked like an old manor house and, as the gates had been left open, he decided to drive through them and along the winding driveway until he had reached the old house itself. From the very moment he had reached the fork in the road, John had been overwhelmed with feelings that he could only describe as déjà vu.

Now the old manor house itself seemed uncannily familiar, even though he had never visited this part of the country before. As he climbed wearily from his car, he seemed to have a sense of "knowing" exactly where he was. Even the five stone steps up to the ornately carved oak doors seemed so familiar and, for a moment, his thoughts drifted back to the days when the house was first built.

John had always had an affinity for this historical period and had always nurtured a strong desire to collect pieces of furniture from that time.

Pat, however, had more modern tastes and despised anything that was older than she was, so he had never been able to indulge in his passion.

John had intended to ask the people in the house for some assistance, or perhaps allow him to stay there, at least until the fog had lifted sufficiently for him to resume his journey. As he ascended the stone steps, he could see that the old place was in darkness and was probably unlived in.

He reached out for the heavy metal knocker and the door swung open, with no more than a little shove. As John entered the hallway, he was immediately overwhelmed by the musty smells and cold damp atmosphere associated with empty houses and he quickly surmised that nobody had lived there for quite some time.

Before venturing further into the house, he called out to make quite certain that it was empty. His voice echoed through the darkness, and seemed to rebound from wall to wall. But, although the old place was eerie, he did not feel uncomfortable or afraid in any way whatsoever.

He found an old oil lamp that still contained a small amount of oil and, after several attempts, he managed to light it. All the time he seemed to be guided by some deep-rooted instinct, as he systematically wended his way through the empty house from room to room.

He seemed to be quite familiar with the architectural layout and was quite surprised to discover that he knew exactly where the kitchen was situated. He could not understand why the old house was so familiar, or why he was experiencing a strange feeling of excitement in the pit of his stomach, almost as though he had come home. He was so preoccupied with the search that he had quite forgotten the reason he was there in the first place.

John was certain that the fog was there for the night and since he was so unperturbed by his surroundings, he'd decided to find a comfortable chair in which to settle down for the night. Although the old manor house had obviously been empty for some time, all the furniture was still in place, covered with white, protective dust sheets. John snuggled down on a large, plush settee and, in no time at all had fallen fast asleep.

He woke up just before six o'clock in the morning and, although it was still fairly dark outside, he could see the moon shining through the window at the top of the stairs and therefore knew that the fog had cleared. His night spent in the unheated house had left him feeling stiff and chilled and he could not wait to get home. Pat would be worried sick and he would have to find a telephone box as soon as possible to let her know that he was alright.

The silvery light of the moon illuminated the room and he could now see the fireplace quite clearly. Its ornate surround still had the manor house's original family crest in pride of place, and the name, *John Barrington Moore* was etched in its centre. John went cold as he read the name and many images flashed quickly through his mind. The name was so familiar and seemed to jog some ancient memory within him. His mind seemed to be flooded with images and thoughts of days gone by. John had a passion for history and he was sure that he had read somewhere that John Barrington Moore had been hanged for murder in the nineteenth century. He could not quite remember where exactly he had read it, but he definitely, somehow, recalled the name. For some unknown reason, this made him feel quite unsettled and he wanted to leave at once.

As soon as John was seated in his car and had started the engine, he could feel his heart pounding inside his chest. He turned the vehicle round in front of the house and accelerated quickly down the gravel driveway, glancing nervously in the mirror as he sped through the gates, leaving the imposing old house behind him. The whole episode occupied his mind to such an extent on the way home that he completely forgot to phone Pat to let her know that he was safe and well.

John's stay in the old manor house was the sole topic of conversation for over a week and he knew that his wife did not believe a word of his story. And so, on a bright Sunday afternoon, two weeks after the New Year, he decided to take a drive with her and the children to find the old house.

It was a beautiful clear day and, to John's great surprise, he was able to drive straight to the old manor house that had been his safe retreat on the foggy night, without getting lost once. He drove through the gates and along the winding driveway towards the front entrance, with the same rush of excitement quickening his heart that he had felt on that dismal foggy night. He was looking forward to seeing the imposing edifice once again, this time in full daylight and he wanted to prove to Pat, once and for all, that he had been telling her the truth. But he was in for a nasty shock.

As the car emerged from the driveway and edged towards the front of the house, he could not believe what he was seeing. Before him was only a shell of a house, silhouetted against the clear blue sky; its fire-charred walls now decaying beneath the winds of time. Although the grounds had obviously been well-kept, with geometrically landscaped gardens front and rear, the house itself looked as though it had been a victim of the bombing raid in the Second World War.

"Some house!" scoffed Pat sarcastically. "And I suppose you're now going to tell me that this is not the place?"

John pulled the car to a halt and just sat in stunned silence, unable to respond to his wife's remark. Then somebody tapped on the side window and he turned his head to see an elderly man standing there smiling at him.

"Nice to see you again, Mr. Barrington Moore," the man grinned, with a sudden look of embarrassment as

John turned to face him. "Oh! I do beg your pardon, sir," he said. "I thought you were Mr. Barrington Moore."

John felt an icy shiver pass right through him, as though someone had walked across his grave. He climbed out of the car, eager to speak to the old man.

"I'm the gardener here, sir," he explained. "I've been looking after these gardens since I left school, some sixty years ago."

"The house..." John stammered. "What's happened to the house?"

"Oh, the house was burnt down in the late nineteenth century," explained the old man. "The family like to keep the gardens maintained."

John went even colder and could not believe the information he had just been given. He knew that he had stayed there on that foggy night and had looked around the old house and seen the fireplace with the name inscribed on its surrounds.

"That's not possible!" he replied in a daze. "I came here..."

He stopped suddenly and turned to face the old manor house and the old man could see the puzzled expression in his eyes.

"John Barrington Moore murdered his uncle in a fit of rage," explained the old man. "He then set fire to the house in an attempt to destroy all the evidence. Nonetheless, he was convicted and hanged six months later." The man paused for a moment, while John absorbed what he had told him. But John had known that already. He had remembered it when he was looking around the house, particularly when he saw the fireplace.

"You're the spitting image of the present Mr. John Barrington Moore. The spitting image you are," the gardener went on.

John found the whole experience a little too bizarre to take in. He felt unable to tell Pat the whole incredible story, because he knew she would not believe a word of it. He wanted to tell his wife that he believed that he was John Barrington Moore, but he knew she would just laugh at him.

"What was the name of the uncle who was murdered?" he asked.

"Charles Barrington Moore," the man replied. "He was extremely wealthy and his nephew, John Barrington Moore, lived in this house with his uncle."

John was intrigued by the whole story and wanted to find out all he could about the Barrington Moore family.

"Why did he murder his uncle?"

"He threatened to cut his nephew out of his will," enthused the old man. "John Barrington Moore was a gambling man and had lost all his money. After killing his uncle he burned the house down to cover his misdeeds."

The old gardener bade John farewell and made his way slowly along the path towards the gardens at the rear of the house. John stood there for a moment, pensively watching the retreating figure. It was all coming back to him, image after powerful image, flooding his mind with memories and vivid pictures that he was now somehow being forced to remember.

John never believed in reincarnation, but this was all too much of a coincidence. He was being overwhelmed by strong emotions from the past and for the moment he felt as though he was living in two completely different ages.

"I am John Barrington Moore!" he muttered to himself. "I have returned."

John's thoughts were sharply interrupted by Pat, who was calling him from the car.

"John, can we go now? The kids are starving and the baby's waking up!"

He climbed back into the car with a heavy sigh, overwhelmed by the feeling that he was leaving behind an important part of his past. He reluctantly started the engine and turned the car in front of the house for the last time, before accelerating quickly down the long driveway and through the gates, without glancing back even for a single moment.

He was now certain that he was John Barrington Moore and that, for some reason, he had returned to the house, which he had destroyed. John never returned to the old manor house again, for he had no desire to be hanged for the same crime twice!

TWO

Love

Love transcends the confines of the physical world—it defies logic and even in death love persists. From the unrequited love of our pets, to the love of one person for another, love always finds a way to return. Love is undoubtedly the greatest and most powerful force in the universe and can never be broken, not even by the icy hand of death.

Jenny's Gone Home

The Ansons all agreed that the family's new German Shepherd dog should be called "Jenny," a suitable name for an extremely friendly creature with an agreeable and loving nature. Although Jenny had been bought as a pet for the children, Sydney was quite surprised when the family's new addition seemed to attach herself to him, and followed him everywhere. In fact, the two became inseparable and went everywhere together. When Sydney Anson retired for the night, usually after midnight, Jenny would finish the last of her dinner and then patiently await her loving master's whistle, telling her that it was time for her to join him. Although Jenny was never allowed on the bed, she did sleep on a large cushion next to the dressing table, and even had her own warm duvet. The whole family had now accepted the fact that Jenny was their father's dog, and they had all become quite accustomed to the familiar whistle just after midnight.

The years went by and Sidney Anson was diagnosed with terminal cancer. Being the loving family man that he was, he insisted that he should spend his last weeks at home with his family. He would frequently be found sitting on the stairs struggling for breath, his faithful companion sitting by his side. Although everyone was deeply saddened when Sydney finally lost his battle against his illness, Jenny found it very difficult to function without her loving master. She wouldn't eat and very quickly went into a deep depression. The vet had warned the family that they should not expect Jenny to live any longer than a few days. Sydney's daughter, Jane, nursed Jenny in front of the fire, and on the very evening she drew her last breath, Jane heard the unmistakable sound of her father whistling from upstairs, just as he always did when he called her to bed. Jane's mother also heard it, and her brother who was usually a heavy sleeper, quickly came downstairs to see if everyone else had heard it. At least now the grieving family was comforted to know that their father was alright, and that he and Jenny were now together. "Jenny has gone home, mum," smiled Jane to her mother. "She's with dad again."

I Just Called to Say I Love You

Steve and David Shelton were absolutely devastated when their mother, Sue, died after a long battle with cancer. The death of their father four years before had made the family very close and now they were going through the same painful experience again.

Although Sue didn't want to die, she had to be practical about the whole horrible thing. Once she had put all her affairs in order, she made it clear to her two sons exactly what she wanted—to be allowed to die with dignity in her own home.

Sue had spent the whole of her working life as a nurse, so she knew more or less what to expect when the end came. Her only concern was for her boys to be prepared and be able to cope when she had gone. She prayed that they would be strong enough to cope when she became too frail to function.

Whilst Steve was the eldest at twenty, nineteen-year-old David was far more mature and never really showed his feelings. Steve was Sue's main concern, and she just hoped they would help each other through the distressing ordeal.

Although Sue had been given six months to live by her consultant, she sadly fell into decline within four months and became so ill that she was unable to get out of bed. Her two devoted sons made her as comfortable as possible and even installed an intercom system to make her last days a little easier for her.

Sue passed away peacefully early one September Sunday morning, and although her death was expected, Steve and David were devastated. Two weeks after the funeral, the brothers were in the living room sorting through some of their mother's papers when they heard the intercom buzzer resound through the house. They both froze and stared at each other.

Although the intercom system was still in place, it had been disconnected from its power source shortly after Sue had died. Thinking that they had somehow imagined it all, they dismissed the eerie sound of the intercom and continued to sort through their mother's papers.

The buzzer sounded again, only this time with more urgency. Staring anxiously at his brother at his brother, Steve reluctantly went into the kitchen where the intercom sat on the table by the window. The buzzer resounded once again, and he quickly and yet nervously lifted the receiver to his ear. His heart missed several beats as he heard his mother's unmistakable voice say, "I love you both."

The phone then went silent. Steve felt numb and knew that his brother would not believe him, and so he decided not to say anything. He felt a warmth inside and was reassured about his mother, and knew that she was now alright.

"What was it?" asked David walking into the room, staring curiously at his brother. "What happened?"

Steve just grinned and shook his head. "The system somehow retained some of its power," he said quickly, without thinking. "That's all!"

"Spooky though?" retorted his brother. "For one moment…"

"Yes, I know," Dave interrupted. "Me too."

The truth was their mother had called to tell her boys that she was alright and that she loved them.

A Mother's Wedding Ring

Holy Trinity church had stood proud over the graveyard for over two hundred years and was a local landmark in the ancient village of Wavertree in the north of England. On a Sunday afternoon, the cemetery was a busy thoroughfare with many people using it as a shortcut to get to the local park just across the road. Apart from this, Holy Trinity was just like any other cemetery, with rows and rows of graves, some straight and well-cared for, and others with headstones ravaged by time and many upturned by vandals. May Rogers had visited Holy Trinity every week after her mother had died five years before and had always found it to be quiet and peaceful. Her eight-year-old son, Michael, always accompanied her and would always amuse himself whilst his mother tidied the grave. Then he'd fetch water from the nearby tap while mother arranged the flowers in the pot. Although Michael always found the trip to the cemetery boring, it was a weekly ritual he put up with for his mother's sake. It was March 1990 and, because Michael was going to his cousin's birthday party, they had gone to the cemetery in the morning instead of the usual time in the afternoon. As soon as they arrived, May quickly set about tidying the grave, and Michael went to fetch the water for the flowers. Whilst he was filling the pot with water he noticed a lady standing beside him, waiting to use the tap, he thought. She smiled at him. "Hello Michael," she said warmly, "You've grown into a fine young man, haven't you?" Thinking that she must be someone who knew his mother, he smiled politely back at her, and then turned to make his way back to the grave. "Michael," the woman said, holding out her hand to him. "Give your mother this. It belongs to her." The young boy held out his hand, and the woman dropped a gold wedding ring into his palm. He closed his fingers tightly around the ring, and thinking no more about it, quickly thanked the lady, and then made his way back to his mother.

"Where have you been, slow coach?" she asked, shaking her head impatiently. "I've been waiting for the water."

"I've been speaking to the nice lady," he said, holding out the ring to his mother. "She said to give you this, that it belongs to you."

His mother's eyes widened as she took the ring from her son's palm. With a puzzled look on her face she examined the ring closely, mouthing the worn inscription inside the gold band. "Ron and Margaret—12. 4. 41." She couldn't believe that she was actually holding her mother's wedding ring. It had been left on her mother's hand and buried with her. May had often wished that she had kept it, just as her mother had wanted. But Ron, her older brother, had insisted that it be left on his mother's hand. She swung round to see the lady her son had been speaking to, but there was nobody there.

"She was there, honest, Mum," Michael insisted. "She did give me the ring. I'm not lying."

May could see that her son was quite upset, and so she placed a reassuring hand on his head. "I know, son. I believe you."

She smiled to herself, and felt an icy-cold shiver pass right through her, as she lowered her eyes to her mother's grave. "Thanks, Mum," she whispered. "I love you."

A Daughter's Love Knows No Bounds

Speaking as someone who was born and bred in Liverpool, England, during the 1950s and 1960s, I have to say that it has changed in many ways beyond recognition. I was brought up in Grosvenor Road in the Wavertree area of Liverpool, in a two-up and two-down terraced house with no bathroom and an outside toilet. Nonetheless, as anyone who lived in Wavertree in the fifties and sixties will affirm, the close-knit community was extremely friendly with ever-open front doors and no fear of being burgled. Everybody knew everybody's business, and the whole community's camaraderie was what made Liverpool so strong during the so-called Blitz of the Second World War. Even though the German bombers were systematically devastating the city of Liverpool in 1942, the spirit of the people and their survival instinct remained strong and relentless. Growing up in the 1950s, visible signs of the war were still apparent everywhere, and there was not a street, or even a single house that did not bear the scars of the bombing. In fact, in many areas, only desolation could be seen and the war-scarred streets of Wavertree where Ken Luxton was born and had lived all his life, stood as a reminder that the whole country was under siege.

On one particular awful night, bombs had fallen more or less constantly and had devastated houses in Ash Grove, Ashfield, and Wavertree Vale. Ken Luxton had been helping search for survivors in the debris of a house in Ash Grove, where he also lived, and had stopped to drink a welcome cup of tea, which was being served by a group of locals at a makeshift roadside canteen.

Ken stood pensively in complete silence, his eyes solemnly scanning the desolation before him, in horror and disbelief, only vaguely aware of the sounds around him, when he felt someone tugging insistently at his arm. He lowered his eyes to see a little girl with her hair in pigtails and the biggest blue eyes that he had ever seen. She was distressed and crying almost hysterically as she pulled at his arm in an attempt to get him to follow her.

"Wait a minute, love," said Ken kindly, stooping to speak to her at her own height. "Now then, dry those eyes and tell me what's wrong?"

"My mummy is trapped in the cellar of our house," she sobbed. "Please help her. She can't move."

"Right!" said Ken urgently. "But first of all, tell me your name?"

"Linda," she sobbed. "Linda Goreman."

"Okay, Linda," he continued. "My name is Ken. I want you to show me exactly where your mummy is and we'll have her out in no time."

Without another word being spoken, the little girl ran off through the debris at the corner of Ash Grove, pausing for a moment to make sure that Ken was close behind. He followed her into the back entrance of the corner grocer's shop and along the alleyway leading into Wavertree Vale. She stopped abruptly by the remains of what had once been a house at the corner of the entry and urgently beckoned Ken to the spot. He could see immediately that the building had been reduced to rubble in the previous night's raid and doubted if anyone could possibly have survived such an impact.

"She's in there," cried the little girl. "My mummy's trapped in the cellar with Laddie, my doggie. Please help them. Please get them out."

Ken paused for a moment whilst his eyes surveyed the devastation before him and, despite his pessimistic assessment, he tried to reassure her.

"Don't worry, love, your mummy and doggie will be alright. We'll have them out in no time. Just stand over there so you won't get hurt should any of the rubble fall."

Helped by two other men, Ken picked his way cautiously towards the entrance to the cellar, scrambling over the bricks and debris, pausing for a moment to check that the little girl was at a safe distance. He could see that she was waiting anxiously at the roadside and so continued to claw his way forward. There was no question that the house had taken a direct hit, which usually meant no survivors. The men's task seemed almost futile, but Ken knew that he just had to continue for the little girl's sake.

He could never have done it by himself and was so grateful that he had someone helping him to clear the bricks and huge slabs of concrete that were blocking his way into the cellar. But time was now of the essence if there was to be any hope at all of a successful rescue.

Losing all track of time, the men dug furiously and Ken completely forgot about the little girl. As the minutes turned into hours, Ken's clothes became stuck to his body with sweat and he ached so much that he felt as though he was about to collapse.

But just when he thought that he could continue no longer, he detected a muffled voice followed by a dog barking coming from beneath the rubble. Ken gestured for the other two men to stop digging and be quiet so that he could listen, but all he could hear was the occasional sound of falling bricks and cracking timber. They were just about to resume their search, when Ken heard the voice again followed by a dog whimpering.

"Please, please help me ..."

Ken lowered his ear to the place where he thought the sound was coming from and then he yelled as loudly as he could.

"Keep shouting!" he urged. "Keep shouting so that I can work out exactly where to dig."

"Please help me," came the woman's voice again. "Help me."

Along with the dog excitedly barking, the men more or less knew the woman's exact location. The woman's voice seemed to get louder each time she called out, making her rescuers even more determined to dig her free. Within minutes, the men had somehow cleared a way into the cellar and had pulled the woman and the dog clear of the rubble and out into the daylight. Although very badly shaken, aside from a few scratches and bruises, Linda's mother was basically unharmed and was hugely relieved to see her rescuer's smiling faces and to be out in the fresh air once again.

"Thank God!" she gasped, as Ken helped her to pick her way unsteadily over the rubble to the pavement. "Thank God you saved me and my dog. How on earth did you know I was down there?"

Ken laughed, overcome with emotion and understandable pride at their life-saving achievement.

"Nobody would ever have known you were there, had it not been for your little girl!" and he smiled broadly and turned to look for Linda.

"Little girl?" said the woman, puzzled. "What little girl?"

"Your little girl," retorted Ken excitedly, suddenly wondering if the woman had been concussed in the bombing.

"What did she look like?" asked the woman, intrigued.

"Oh, about so high," said Ken, indicating the girl's height with his hand. "She had two pigtails and the biggest blue eyes I have ever seen. She said her name was Linda."

A tear suddenly trickled down the woman's cheek, cutting a little river through the dust and grime that covered her from head to toe as the little girl's name fell almost silently from her lips.

"Linda!" she whispered, a slight trembling smile parting her lips. "My little girl. She was killed in the first twelve months of the war."

"But I saw her with my own eyes," insisted Ken, an icy chill passing through him. "I actually spoke to her and touched her."

"My Linda!" repeated the woman, obviously shocked. "My precious little girl…"

Destination Unknown

June Parry was devastated when Richie, her husband, had died of a heart attack at the relatively young age of fifty-three. He had been her constant companion since she was seventeen, and now she was all alone. Her only son was working in America, and although he came home as often as his work allowed, she still felt sad and lonely.

Richie had been a computer enthusiast and had also fancied himself a writer. He knew that he was not talented enough to be a successful author, but this did not stop him from writing prodigiously. He had enjoyed writing so much that he would sometimes stay up until the early hours of the morning, lost in his own little world of fantasy and fiction. Now June was left alone with her memories and the remains of her husband's dreams and aspirations.

Although June was quite religious and attended church regularly every Sunday, Richie had been a lifelong agnostic and always joked that people who went to church were simply hedging their bets, or playing safe, "just in case."

"Well," June always protested to her husband, "where do you think we all go when we die?"

"Destination unknown, Captain Kirk," he would always answer sarcastically. "Destination unknown!"

Richie had now been dead for six months and June was sitting quietly in front of his computer, composing an email to her son in America. Suddenly, her husband came into her mind and her thoughts began to wander. She found herself thinking about all the good times that she and Richie had enjoyed together and was suddenly overwhelmed with grief and loss.

A few minutes elapsed and June eventually collected her thoughts and composed herself sufficiently to continue writing the email to her son. After she had written a few more sentences, she paused for a moment and stared sadly at the computer screen, her thoughts turning to her dead husband once more. She wondered what most people in her position wonder, "Where is Richie now?" And almost in that moment, June noticed that someone had sent her an email. She naturally assumed that it was from her son and immediately clicked the box to read it.

It simply read: "DESTINATION UNKNOWN—I LOVE YOU."

No one but June had known what Richie used to say, so now she knew that he was fine—wherever he was.

The Sins of the Fathers

Barbara Dutton's eighteen-year-old son, Michael, had been on his way home from a party when he had been murdered.

She knew she would never get over his untimely, horrific death, but she did hope that the pain would eventually get a little easier. At first, the murder had placed an enormous strain on her marriage, but ten years on, Barbara's relationship with her husband, Pete, was much stronger than ever. Their only consolation was that Michael's killer, Bob Carter, had been tried in court, prosecuted, and given a life sentence.

It was 1989, and the couple had moved into a new house a couple of weeks before Christmas and now they both wanted to put the past behind them. They had made their plans for the New Year and had already arranged for a local company to install a new kitchen at the beginning of January. As far as the Duttons were concerned, this was to be a new beginning.

Once the kitchen fitters had moved in, Barbara began to make arrangements for the new furniture to be delivered. She had decided that everything was going to be just perfect. Both Barbara and Peter had always been very particular about allowing workmen into their home, but the kitchen fitters were clean and very polite and seemed very trustworthy.

Whilst Peter was at work, Barbara supplied them with endless cups of tea and biscuits. She found one of the young men particularly amiable and easy to talk to. During their tea break one morning, Barbara engaged in conversation with the young man, and asked him whether he was married. He told her that he had been married for five years and that his wife was expecting their second child in March.

"Do you have any other family?" she inquired. "Are your parents still alive?"

The young man fell silent and seemed a little uncomfortable with Barbara's question.

"My mother died two years ago," he said sadly. "And my father..." he suddenly stopped, moved awkwardly in his seat and looked quite extremely nervous. "My father's, erm...in prison."

It was quite obvious to Barbara that he did not want to discuss it any further, so she decided to quickly change the subject.

"You must be really excited about the baby," she said. "Not long to go now!"

But the young man appeared not to have heard what she had said and muttered in a low voice, "He murdered someone!"

"Your father murdered someone?" gasped Barbara. "How awful!"

"Yes, it was horrible," nodded the young man. "He stabbed a young guy to death ten years ago."

A strange sensation washed over Barbara and for a moment she was unable to speak. She wasn't quite sure what the feeling was, but she knew that as the young man spoke his words had overwhelmed her.

"What is your father's name?" she asked, almost incoherently, somehow predicting what the answer would be.

"Bob Carter," came the reply. "You won't know him. I wish I didn't know him either."

"I know him alright," snapped Barbara, her voice suddenly sounding cold and hard. "He murdered my son, Michael Jameson. He was only eighteen."

For a brief moment her eyes locked onto the young man's and all her sadness came rushing back. But then she realised that this was more than pure coincidence—that there really was no such thing as coincidence. She noted the anguish in the young man's eyes and in that moment she knew that all her pain was over. In this case, the sins of the father had truly been passed to the son. Barbara knew full well that it was not the young man's fault, and a slight smile parted her lips as she warmly touched his hand.

This was surely one of life's unexplainable coincidences that was perhaps organised by a greater supernatural power, possibly to allow the ghost of things that have been to be laid to rest.

Terence Came to Say Goodbye

Because of a serious respiratory disease I had developed at the age of three, I was sent to a school for children with life-threatening illnesses. As I wasn't a rough-and-tumble kid, I felt quite comfortable there with kids who were just like me.

No one ever knew exactly what the other kids suffered with; all that we ever knew about each other was that everyone at the school suffered with some sort of lung problem. As far as all the kids were concerned, we all shared a common bond.

Terence Davies knew very well that he was bigger and stronger than most of the kids, and as a result he was feared by everyone. He was a bully, but for some unknown reason he befriended me and always wanted to spend time with me. We were very close and played together, ate our lunch together, and shared our weekly comics.

I have been mediumistically inclined since I was a child, and seeing so-called "dead" people was commonplace to me—and I really did think all kids were the same as me. I could always see that Terence was somehow quite special. Not just because he was protective towards me, but he had an unusual aura about him. Although he was a boy of few words, he did seem to spend a lot of time contemplating things and would always question what the teacher said.

We never kept in touch over the weekend or during the school holidays, so it was always good to see him when we were back at school.

Although Terence didn't look particularly ill, he suddenly went absent from school. One week went into two weeks, then two weeks into four. He was off school for ten weeks, and then one Monday morning when we were preparing for Morning assembly and prayers I saw Terence on the far side of the playground. I was so glad to see my friend but was puzzled why he didn't come over to see me. He looked different, pale and much thinner. He kept his distance and just smiled and waved. As he made no attempt to come to see me, I began to make my way towards him, but before I could the bell went calling us into religious assembly. Because Terence Davies was of a different religious faith to me he had to go to a different prayer assembly. Before assembly began the teacher announced: "This morning we must mention Terence Davies in our prayers. Terence passed away in hospital over the weekend after a long illness."

I'd seen him as clear as day at the far side of the playground. He smiled and waved to me. Nobody else in the school saw him. It was then that I realised my friend only came to say goodbye.

Little Tommy Remembers

After five disappointing years of trying to have a baby, Lyn Fairfax joyfully announced to her husband, Tom, that she was pregnant. They were so happy they couldn't wait to tell Tom's parents and her mother, who now lived alone after the death of her father twelve months before.

Six years had passed by and their five-year-old son, Tommy, had just started school. Because he wasn't a "rough-and-tumble" child, Lyn found herself being very protective towards him. He was an extremely sensitive little boy and showed no interest at all in football or any of the other sporting activities many children his age participated in.

Because of Lyn's tuition, her son could read exceptionally well and would spend most of his time with his head buried in a book. He appeared very advanced for his age, and would often come out with the most profound statements, mystifying his parents, who wondered where on earth their little boy had come from.

After collecting Tommy from school one blustery and very cold Friday afternoon, Lyn made her way to the village to collect her husband's suit and her winter coat from the dry cleaner. As she helped her son from the car, he blurted, "Where's Mason's bakery gone?"

Lyn stopped and looked at her son in disbelief. She thought she had misheard him and so asked him to repeat what he had said.

"Where's Mason's bakery gone?"

Mason's bakery had in fact been demolished just before her son had been born and Lyn knew full well that he couldn't possibly have known about it.

"How do you know Mason's bakery?" she asked him. "You weren't even born!"

A broad smile dawned across Tommy's lips, and he gave his mother a knowing look. "I'm your father!" he announced in a matter-of-fact voice. "Of course I remember Mason's bakery, silly!"

Lyn felt a cold shiver pass through her body as she gazed at her son's little face. She could see he was very serious and knew that he was far too young to be playing games.

Before Lyn could utter another word, Tommy took his mother's hand and grinned cheekily. "Come on, Babs," he said quietly. "We'll have to buy our chocolate cupcakes somewhere else."

Lyn was suddenly overwhelmed with sadness. Her son could not have known that her father called her Babs right up until the day he died, and that as a child he always bought her chocolate cupcakes when he collected her from school.

I knew the Fairfax family well, and Tommy never said anything like that ever again.

The Train that Never Came

It was 1968 and George Ashcroft, who had now worked for the railway for over twenty years, had been transferred to Wellington Road station in the suburbs of Liverpool, England, one of the city's quieter railway stations. George's transfer was a blessing in disguise; the station was not only quiet, but it also closed at midnight every night. And because he only worked the late shift twice a week, he had far more time to spend with his family. Although he had to work late on his first week, he didn't mind, as this gave him the opportunity to get to know the other two porters working at the station.

It was 10:00 p.m. on Monday and his two colleagues had gone for their tea break. George was brushing some discarded sweet wrappers from the platform and generally tidying up when he noticed a young woman in her twenties standing there alone and looking pale and quite lost. Not wanting to make his concern too obvious, he began to brush around where she was standing. "Why don't you make yourself more comfortable," he said, smiling warmly, "and sit on the bench? After all, that's what it's for." He swept his hand across the seat, brushing away all the grime, and gesturing for her to sit down.

"I'm okay," she answered, not taking her eyes from the in-coming railway line. "I'm waiting for my husband. He's coming home tonight."

George couldn't help but notice how unusually dressed the young woman was, quite fashionable but in the style of the 1940s. The only time she actually looked at George was to thank him for his kindness. Thinking no more about it, he went about his business of getting the station ready for the last two trains, 10:30 p.m. and 11:30 p.m. By the time his colleagues had returned to their duty, George himself was parched and ready for his well-earned cup of tea, the last break before clocking off duty for the night. By the time he had returned, there were still a few people waiting for the last train to arrive at 11.30 p.m., usually right on the dot. As the young woman was no longer there, he assumed that she had collected her husband and had gone home.

The following night was George's last night on the late shift. As he was a man of routine and liked to keep things clean and tidy, as always he set about the job of brushing the platform. He stopped to scrape some discarded chewing gum from the concrete surface when he noticed the young woman from the previous night, standing there, as before, alone. He pulled himself slowly to his feet and walked over to her. "Hello again," he smiled. "I thought your husband was coming home last night?"

This time the young woman just stared at the in-coming train line, appearing completely oblivious to him even being there. "Are you alright?" he asked, concerned. But again she ignored him. Not wanting to disturb her any longer, George turned to make his way to the other side of the platform. He felt a little sorry for the young woman and wondered what was wrong with her. Upon reaching the trash can on the far side of the platform, a short distance from the entrance, he turned to look back at the woman, but to George's surprise she had gone—disappeared into thin air. He knew that to leave the station she would have had to have passed him. He checked all through the station but there was absolutely no sign of her.

The young woman's disappearance concerned George Ashcroft so much, she was on his mind for days. It was only when he discussed her with one of his colleagues that her mystery was solved.

"That's Mary Phillips," said his friend. "You've seen a ghost, George!"

"What do you mean?" he gasped. "Ghosts don't hold conversations."

"Are you sure about that, George?" His colleague laughed. "You're not the first to talk to her, and I'm sure you won't be the last!"

"There are no such things as ghosts!" huffed George. "I know what I saw, and she was not a ghost!"

"When I first came to work here, I had the same experience," the man reminisced. "Very much in the same way as you, but unlike you she disappeared right before my eyes. I couldn't believe it." He went on to explain that during World War II, many troops would arrive at Wellington Road Railway Station to be met by their wives and girlfriends. He went on to say that Mary Phillips was a newly married local girl. Her husband was due home in 1943 but was killed when the plane he was travelling in crashed into the English Channel.

"She must have been heartbroken!" lamented George. "How sad!"

"But at least she spoke to you, George," said his colleague. "She obviously felt comforted that you were concerned for her."

George Ashcroft solemnly shook his head. "But the train she was waiting for never arrived. That is so sad!"

Glitter from Heaven

Beverly Scott had been devastated when her friend Jan had died at the age of thirty-seven after a short and very distressing illness.

Jan had left two young children and her husband, Andrew, who had gone into a deep depression and no longer wanted to live. Beverly tried everything to encourage him to get on with his life, but without the woman he had been with since he was fourteen, life no longer had any meaning.

Had it not been for the children, Beverly was certain that Andrew would have ended his own life. His world had been turned upside down and he was now so unhappy that he had to force himself to climb out of bed in the morning. Beverly and her husband, Phil, kept in touch with Andrew as much as they possibly could and occasionally invited him to their home for meals.

As the months passed by, everyone was quite pleased to see that Andrew was slowly beginning to put his life back together again, and was already planning to take the children on holiday to the coast. Although he still missed his wife very much, the hurt was definitely beginning to ease.

After a hard day at work, Beverly went to bed early on the Friday night and quickly fell into a deep sleep. She dreamt that her friend visited her to say thank you for all she had done and to tell her that she was alright. In the dream, the two friends embraced and then Beverly watched tearfully as Jan bade her farewell. As she faded into the distance silver glitter cascaded down upon Beverly and at that very moment she woke up. It was now morning and the sun flooded the room. It was a beautiful day and Beverly felt an overwhelming sense of peace. Knowing that her friend was happy she couldn't wait to tell Jan's husband about her dream.

At that moment, her husband Phil appeared at the door with a cup of coffee and some toast, placing the tray carefully on the bed beside his wife. Beverly was eager to tell him about her dream but before she could speak he said: "What's all that in your hair?" He brushed Beverly's hair with his hand and silver glitter fell onto the duvet.

Beverly smiled and wiped a single tear from her eye. "Jan," she whispered. "It wasn't a dream after all."

"What is it?" asked Phil puzzled, brushing some of the glitter onto the palm of his hand. "Where did that come from?"

Beverly smiled. "From heaven," she muttered thoughtfully. "It's glitter from heaven."

Who's Nelly?

Nelly Baxter had been a dear friend for more than twenty years, and I really loved her like a mother. At seventy-six, she was everyone's mother and over the years had fostered countless children, who always visited her for many years after, even when they had families of their own.

Nelly was always there for me whenever I had a problem and even when I didn't, I always made it my business to call and see her at least twice a week. In fact, I always made it my business to call on Nelly for a cup of tea and a chat whenever I was passing her place, and there was always a warm welcome for me. Although Nelly Baxter wasn't actually housebound, she was in poor health and had to go to the hospital every week for dialysis treatment. She had been on the waiting list for a kidney transplant for three years, but at the age of seventy-six she wasn't regarded as a "priority," and unfortunately, Nelly passed away of a heart attack whilst undergoing treatment. Hundreds of people came from far and wide to her funeral, and it came as no surprise to me to discover just how many people she actually did help during her lifetime.

When Nelly died, my son, Ben, was only three months old. Nelly doted on him and used to take him to the park in his pram right up until the day she died.

When Ben was three years old, I was driving home with him and had to pass Nelly Baxter's house. I was nostalgically recalling how I used to call on her uninvited and there would always be a welcoming cup of tea and a sandwich. I was thinking if she was still alive how she would have loved me to have called with him. Ben was an extremely quiet child and never spoke a lot. But we had just passed Nelly's home when he said "Who's Nelly, Daddy?"

I went cold as an icy chill quickly passed through me and I pulled the car to halt at the sidewalk. "Why do you ask that, Ben?" I stuttered. "What made you ask who Nelly is?"

He looked at me with his large brown eyes, and said quite nonchalantly, "My head is speaking to me." He pointed to his head, and then turned to look out of the car window, completely unconcerned.

I never really knew whether Ben had telepathically tuned in to what I was thinking or whether he had received some sort of communication from Nelly Baxter herself. Whatever or whoever caused him to hear Nelly's name, that was no isolated incident. It happened on several occasions after that, and Ben always gave the same answer, "My head is speaking to me."

Although Ben has never made any reference to those experiences since then, today at twenty-nine years old he is an accomplished musician and extremely sensitive. I have never had any doubt at all that he is and always has been mediumistically inclined and will hopefully one day accept that.

THREE

Ghosts

Walking through the city centre on a busy Saturday afternoon, the majority of us pay little or no attention to the hundreds of faces that pass us by. Little do we realize that any one of those faces may very well belong to someone not of this world. There is very little doubt that the "dead" frequently walk beside us unnoticed, very often as unaware of our presence as we are of theirs. Whether they are as interested in us as we are in them is a question that only they can answer. However, there are times when they reach out from beyond their world to help or reassure us, or simply to astound us!

The Vanishing Couple

Most ghostly encounters occur when you least expect them. In fact, if you watch for them, they very rarely happen. People frequently say to me "I've never seen anything!" However, the truth is, how do they know? A paranormal experience can be so spontaneous, that nine times out of ten we don't even notice it. For example, in parapsychology there is a phenomenon often referred to as the "corner of the eye" syndrome. This is when we are sitting down relaxing in our home alone, perhaps completely oblivious to anything but the article we are reading in the evening newspaper, when suddenly we see something out of the corner of our eye. Of course, when we swing round to look, nothing is there! This phenomenon is far more common than we imagine, and one that is frequently dismissed as either tiredness or a trick of light.

In my experience as a medium, I have found that ghostly apparitions can appear to be quite solid and tangible and may sometimes be quite warm to touch.

This is an account of something that happened several years ago to an elderly couple returning from their son's wedding anniversary celebration some miles from their home.

On this particular winter's night in the torrential rain, Derek and Barbara McConlon were driving along an extremely wet and blustery bypass towards the main highway when they came upon a young couple, looking quite cold and drenched, standing miserably at the side of the road trying to hitch a lift. Normally, seventy-year-old Derek wouldn't dream of stopping for anyone, particularly so late at night, but Barbara was very persuasive and argued that they looked like nice people and it would be a kind gesture to give them a lift on such a cold and wet night.

So, reluctantly Derek pulled into the side of the road and the couple clambered gratefully into the back of the warm car. They thanked Derek and Barbara profusely and immediately gave their names as Tricia and Dave Egerton. It was 1969 and the couple explained that they had been to a wedding in a nearby town and had missed the last train home.

By the time they had reached the end of the bypass, on the approach to town where the couple said they lived, the polite conversation between the four of them had been fully exhausted and a rather embarrassing silence had descended upon the car. As they were driving along the main highway, Derek coughed awkwardly and then asked, "Where can I drop you off?"

His question met with total silence, and so thinking that they had fallen asleep, he glanced in the rearview mirror—only to see that nobody was there! He immediately slammed on the brakes and the car screeched to a juddering halt.

"What's the matter?" gasped Barbara, grabbing the dashboard in alarm. She had been dozing for the last ten minutes or so and had been jolted awake by the sudden braking. She looked across at her husband and was immediately struck by his shocked expression. She turned her head to see what he was looking at through the mirror.

"They've gone!" he stammered in disbelief. "My God! Where are they?"

Barbara immediately climbed out of the car to look back along the rain-drenched main highway, but it was completely deserted.

"I can't understand it!" exclaimed Derek. "They couldn't possibly have jumped out of the car. I was going far too fast. But why would they anyway? Where the bloody hell are they?"

The incident left the couple more than a little mystified and extremely unnerved. They did not know what to think and decided that the whole episode was best forgotten, at least until the following day. By morning their minds would be more or less rested and they would be better able to make sense of the unusual occurrence.

The following day was Sunday and Derek was enjoying his usual lie-in when Barbara suddenly came dashing into the bedroom and spread the morning newspapers on the duvet in front of her husband.

"Look at this!" she said, shaking him awake. "Look at this picture and read the story."

Derek tiredly rubbed the sleep from his eyes and, suddenly noticing his wife's shocked expression, looked at the newspaper and read the headline: *Newly Married Couple,*

Tricia and Dave Egerton Killed on Their Wedding Day in Tragic Accident.

The Disappearing Coach

The anecdotal account of one person's spooky experience very often fails the scrutinising eye of a sceptic, but when several individuals witness the same eerie phenomenon at the same time, it becomes a different matter altogether.

In November 1969, Kevin Boyd and six of his friends were out on his stag night and were making their way from the Lamb Public House in the High Street en route to the Brook House Inn, a popular Liverpool meeting place for many weekend revellers before heading into town. It was just after nine p.m. and the Brook House was to be their last port of call before taking a taxi into town to finish the celebrations in a club.

"Don't you get up to any mischief," warned Barbara, Kevin's bride-to-be. "I want you at the church on time and in one piece."

They had just crossed the road and had begun making their way towards the next hostelry, when a 1940s-style charabanc pulled up a few yards ahead of them. The lads thought that maybe the coach had been to a vintage vehicle exhibition, and after making a few humorous comments, just carried on their conversation and continued on their way. When they had more or less reached where the coach was parked, the driver opened the door and caught their attention. "Excuse me, lads," he called politely in a cockney accent. "Can you direct me to the Brook House boozer?"

It had just begun to rain and as the lads were going to the Brook House any way, they thought this an ideal opportunity to get a free ride. The driver was only too pleased to oblige, and Kevin and his friends eagerly piled in to the charabanc one after the other. The people already seated in the coach were all wearing American air force uniforms. Some had nodded off, obviously weary from a long journey, and the others politely greeted the friends as they made their way to the back of the coach.

"There are plenty of seats at the back, lads," called the driver, whilst Kevin remained standing in the front to give him directions.

"Why are you going to the Brook House?" Kevin enquired. "Some sort of reunion is it?"

"No," the driver solemnly shook his head as he checked the rearview mirror, and then pushed the gear stick into position before the coach pulled away from the curb with a shudder. "Got to collect Hank Greenwood and Jake Peters, two men from the squadron, then we're heading back to their base at Burtonwood."

Kevin turned to look back at his friends and noticed that some of the airmen appeared injured, with bandaged heads and arms in slings. "Some of the lads look in a bad way, don't they?"

"Yeah, but at least they've all got their tickets home now, so they'll be okay!"

Wondering which war the airmen had been injured in, Kevin decided that it must of course be Vietnam. He turned to look back at the men and was touched by the despondent look on all their faces. He felt so grateful not to be in their shoes, and wondered where their lives would take them next.

The coach chugged its way down towards the Penny Lane terminus, before turning right into Smithdown Road.

"This is the famous Penny Lane," Kevin pointed, "you know, of Beatles fame!"

"The Beatles!" the driver retorted quizzically, glancing sideways at Kevin. "What are they? Sounds like some sort of infestation!"

"Blimey, mate!" Kevin laughed. "You're in Liverpool, and you don't know who the Beatles are? Everyone knows the Beatles. Where've you been hiding for the last few years?" Kevin thought he must be joking and said no more about it, and within minutes the charabanc was turning into the Brook House car park.

"Thanks for that, lads," the driver said. "Liverpool's a maze. I'd never have found it. Cheers."

"Have a beer with us, mate?" Kevin said politely, climbing from the coach. "If you've got time, that is?"

"That's a very tempting offer," replied the driver, "but there are fifteen of us, and that's a expensive round, my friend."

"I'm sure we can buy the lads a drink after all they have been through."

He smiled benignly and gestured to the airmen peering at him through the windows. "If you fancy it, we'll see you inside."

By now Kevin's friends had lined the drinks up on the bar and eagerly awaited his arrival.

He had finished his first pint in no time at all and there was still no sign of the coach driver and airmen. So, after some deliberation, Kevin and one of his friends decided to take a look in the car park and perhaps persuade them all to come and join them for a drink.

There was no sign of the charabanc in the car park, or the American airmen. Kevin was puzzled, but just surmised that they had picked up the other men and were now on their way back to their base at Burtonwood.

When the two friends went back inside the pub, more drinks were waiting for them on the bar. An hour passed by and Kevin and his friends were now really feeling the effects of the night's drinking. "I'm going to have to pace myself now lads," said Kevin. "I don't want to be hungover tomorrow. Barb will kill me."

Kevin noticed a large group of veteran soldiers entering the bar; some were just wearing medals, whilst others were fully attired in U.S. Air Force uniforms, obviously for the Remembrance Day celebration which was to take place on the Sunday. He made a point of engaging in conversation with the man who appeared to be in charge of the group and enquired what they were actually doing in the Brook House.

"We've been coming here since the war ended," the man answered in a broad Southern American drawl, a sombre look suddenly dawning across his lined face. "Fourteen of our boys called in to this hostelry for a drink on the way from London to the airbase at Burtonwood." He was clearly saddened by the memory, and paused for a moment before continuing. "They were killed on their way back to the airbase at Burtonwood. After going through the war and sustaining their injuries, they were all killed here in England. We'd just been drinking together here in the Brook House and me and another guy should have got on the coach with them, but we'd met two girls and decided to stay here a little longer. Had we gone with them I wouldn't be here talking to you. We call in every year to raise a glass or two to their memory."

"How were they killed?" asked Kevin thoughtfully. "Was it in an air raid?"

"Hell, no!" replied the man, shaking his head grimly. "They were killed in a head-on collision with the coach they were travelling in."

Kevin suddenly felt an icy chill pass through him as he recalled the coach that had just given him and his friends a lift. "What is your name?" His words came out in no more than an incoherent whisper.

"My name's Hank Greenwood," replied the man, nodding to his friend now sitting with the other veterans. "And that's Jake Peters over there."

A few moments elapsed before Kevin shook the man's proffered hand. "My name's Kevin Boyd," he said politely, forcing himself to speak. The realisation of exactly what had happened had quickly sobered him and removed all the effects of the night's drinking from his brain. He did not know what to make of it all, and politely bade the man farewell before joining his friends at the bar. He now knew that the driver of the coach and the wounded airmen were not going to join him and his friends for a drink. How could they? They were obviously not of this world, and never would be again! Kevin Boyd just had one question to ask—WHY?

The Wedding Ring

Eileen Chapman was having a well-needed cup of coffee with her daughter, Christine, in a local café. They'd just spent a couple of enjoyable hours rummaging through tables of junk at a local Flea Market and were inspecting the contents of a jewellery box Eileen had bought.

Although the box contained nothing of any value, the jewellery box itself had caught Eileen's eye. The beautifully crafted ornamental piece had to be at least seventy years old, thought Eileen, who always had a keen eye for a bargain. As her daughter emptied the rest of the contents of the box onto the table, she noticed a small envelope tucked into one of the pockets of the satin lining.

It contained a lady's wedding ring, engraved with the initials M.B. and the date 7.8.23. As they sipped their coffee and discussed the ring, Frank Burrows, an elderly neighbour of Eileen's, walked into the café. "Thank God I've found you," he said, breathlessly, with a look of relief on his face. "I was told you might be here."

"What is it?" asked Eileen, with some concern and thinking that her husband, John, had had an accident or something. "Sit down. What's wrong?"

The look of relief on the man's face immediately put Eileen at ease and his eyes settled on the jewellery box sitting on the table. "Mavis from the church told me you'd bought my wife's jewellery box," he began. "When I gave it to them I'd forgotten that I'd put her wedding ring in it for safekeeping. I hadn't intended to give the ring as well."

Eileen laughed and retrieved the ring from the jewellery box. "That's alright," she said affectionately, handing the ring to him. "I wondered whose ring it was. It's a good job it was me who bought it and not a total stranger. You'd never have seen the ring again."

The old man thanked Eileen and, placing the ring securely in his pocket he left the café.

"What a coincidence," remarked Eileen. "He was very lucky it was me who bought it. His wife Mary only died last year, and he's so lost without her."

Later, as Eileen and her daughter walked down the street together towards their home not far from the café, they saw an ambulance and a police car outside of Frank Burrows's house.

Eileen's husband, John, was standing on the step talking to the lady who had been looking after Frank since his wife Mary had died.

"What's happened?" asked Eileen. "Is Frank alright?"

"Unfortunately not!" replied her husband. "It looks as though he had a massive heart attack, most probably in the night."

"That's not possible," retorted Eileen, astonished. "He was talking to us earlier in the café." She nervously checked her watch. "Yes, no more than an hour ago." She looked at her daughter for confirmation and she agreed.

"That's not possible," said the woman, solemnly. "I found him around midday." She paused for a moment. "It was sad really. He was clutching his wife's wedding ring in his hand." Eileen went cold as the woman retrieved the ring from her handbag and showed it to her. "I kept it for safekeeping."

Eileen and her daughter were speechless and just looked at each other in total shock. Frank Burrows had obviously come to Eileen after he had died to ask for his wife's wedding ring back. And now, thanks to Eileen, he was at peace.

The Haunted Windmill

At the far end of what is now Berrington Road in a sub-urb of Liverpool, England, there are the foundations of a fifteeth-century windmill that once overlooked a quarry—remnants of a bygone age.

Before the fifteenth-century windmill in Wavertree (one of the oldest parts of Liverpool) was demolished in 1916, its rotating sails were secured so that they would cast a shadow of a cross onto the ground in a feeble attempt to rid the area of a curse that many believed had been placed upon it by an evil spirit living in the quarry. Residents believed that several people killed there had fallen prey to the evil curse and as a result, numerous attempts were made to exorcise the evil force that allegedly pervaded the whole area. When all attempts to rid the cursed location of the evil spirit had failed, the quarry was eventually filled in and for some years, to the delight of the community, nothing further occurred.

Over the last thirty years, area residents have heard the ghostly cries of a young girl in the dead of night, coming from the direction of where the windmill used to stand. The ghostly apparition of a young girl with long hair has also been seen playing in the area and witnesses have claimed that she simply disappears when anyone approaches her.

In the late eighteenth century, eleven-year-old Marga-ret Coots was playing with her brother and friends by the windmill on a blustery March afternoon, when her hair allegedly became entangled in the rotating windmill blades and her neck was broken as she was pulled up by the mechanism.

James Grimshaw is said to have worked at the mill and was killed when a heavy bale fell on him. Several weeks later his son was also killed at the mill in exactly the same way.

Although the ghostly appearance of the little girl is the one most frequently reported, in the mid-1940s witnesses claimed to have seen an old lady wearing a black shawl and smoking a long white clay pipe. She became known as the smoking lady and was believed to be a portent of misfortune. Many locals believe that because so many fatalities have occurred there over the centuries, the whole area where the windmill once stood is cursed, perhaps by the smoking lady, who it is believed was a witch. Legend has it that she had lived a quiet life in a nearby cottage, sometime around the mid-eighteenth century, when she was tormented and ridiculed by the locals. Many still believe to this day that she sought revenge by cursing everybody who lived and worked there. Various other phenomena have been reported over the years, from ghostly apparitions to disembodied cries echoing through the night. Although today many people dismiss the phenomena as being no more than urban myths, I once lived very close to the windmill site and have personally experienced many different phenomena, from disembodied cries to a young girl sitting in the darkness, crying for her "ma."

The Murder of Silas Peet

Silas Peet despised children of all ages. In fact, Silas Peet despised grown-ups too. Nobody liked him very much either, so as far as everybody in the village was concerned, there was no love lost! Silas Peet lived an extremely reclusive life alone in his little cottage at the edge of Marland wood. He was a shoemaker of some excellence and the only cobbler for miles around, which was the only reason he was tolerated at all by his customers. In fact, his father had been the village shoemaker and cobbler before him, and people travelled far and wide to have shoes made by the old man. There were even suggestions that old Silas Peet even made shoes for the young Princess Victoria, heir to the throne of England, and that the old shoemaker had refused to visit the palace to take measurements, insisting that he was far too busy. Apart from all that was known for sure about the old shoemaker, there were suspicions that he was an extremely wealthy man, and because he never trusted banks, there were rumours that he kept all his money in boxes, empty pots, drawers, and cupboards all over his little cottage. However, it was all based on malicious idle gossip put around by people who resented the fact that a cantankerous old miser had a thriving business. Silas Peet did not care what people thought about him, as long as they left him alone to live his life quietly and without bother.

The years were now taking its toll on Silas Peet's aging body, and against his better judgment, he decided to take on an apprentice to ensure that his craft would continue after he himself had died. Silas had no family, and his only sister had died some ten years ago. Besides his failing health, he admitted that apart from money, his shoemaking business was the most important thing in his life, and he now deemed it necessary to employ someone he could trust. Elizabeth Legg cleaned the shop and helped to give it some semblance of order. She had worked for Silas for nearly ten years and only tolerated his temper and bad manners because she desperately needed the few shillings he gave her each week. Elizabeth was now a widow with four children to feed, three of whom were under the age of twelve, and her eldest son, Benjamin, was now seventeen and desperately in need of a job.

"Tell that lad of yours he can come and work for me!" Silas's announcement surprised Elizabeth who couldn't wait to get home to tell her son. "Tell him to be here by eight a.m. prompt on Monday morning," he demanded as she went through the door. "I like punctuality. If he's not here dead on time, I will easily find somebody else."

Young Benjamin was an extremely likeable young man who took to his new job very quickly. Although Silas never said so, it was clear to everyone that he was quite fond of Benjamin and that the lad had great potential. Apart from this, old Silas secretly enjoyed teaching Benjamin a craft that he himself had taken a lifetime to perfect. It was also quite clear to the old man that the boy really enjoyed his work. He was extremely bright, polite, and hard-working, and these, to Silas, were the prerequisites for success, even though he himself had none of these qualities.

Twelve months had gone by and it was Christmas Eve. It had gone past six p.m. and Benjamin was watching Silas intently, patiently waiting for permission to lock up shop and go home. Christmas Eve was like any other day to Silas Peet, and Christmas itself was simply a time when he could not make any money. In fact, the old man always used the Christmas holiday to catch up on any backlog of work, so that come the New Year he could set about the welcome task of making even more money.

As soon as the clock on the wall struck the half hour, Silas slowly raised his head from the leather boot he had been working on for the past hour, and without saying a single word, shuffled his way towards the counter, mumbling incoherently to himself as he did so. He stooped to retrieve the wooden box that held the day's takings and placed it carefully on the scratched, yet shiny, counter. Benjamin watched patiently as the old man slowly pulled back the lid and emptied the contents of the box onto the counter. The boy's eyes fixed intently on Silas Peet's crooked sinewy fingers as they carefully placed the coins into small equal piles, before meticulously counting them onto the counter, a torturous procedure that Benjamin had been subjected to from the very first day of work. Although Benjamin had quickly got used to the nightly ritual, it was Christmas Eve, and he was eager to get home to help his mother prepare things for the festivities. Silas was fully aware of this and seemed to delight in keeping the boy waiting even longer than usual.

He placed one guinea (worth about twenty-one shillings), Benjamin's wage, carefully on top of the counter, and shoved it deliberately across the surface in the boy's direction. Before Benjamin could say anything, the old man surprised him by giving him a further three gold sovereigns, he said, as a show of appreciation for all his hard work.

Such an act of kindness was completely out of character, and Benjamin was understandably speechless. Without saying anything further, Silas Peet gave the lad permission to leave.

Dumfounded, Benjamin thanked the shoemaker, wished him the season's greetings, and then left. The bell above the door jingled twice before falling silent.

After the old man had emptied the day's takings into his pouch and returned the cashbox to its place beneath the counter, he extinguished the two oil lamps either side of the shop, put on his coat and hat before wrapping his scarf carefully around his neck and shoulders to shield him from the winter chill, and then left his shop, finally checking that the door was securely closed.

Silas Peet was a creature of habit and had followed the same procedure every night for the last sixty years. Before making his way home to his cottage at the edge of the wood, not more than a fifteen-minute walk from his shop, as always he called into the Dog and Kettle Inn for a mug of cider, where he reluctantly exchanged one or two pleasantries with some local inhabitants of the village, before finally making his way home.

It was an extremely cold and blustery night, and the winter chill was playing havoc with Silas's arthritic bones. He walked at a leisurely pace from the village and along the winding narrow footpath leading to his little cottage in Marland wood. The moon was bright and the swaying branches of the trees cast eerie, dancing shadows across his path. Although the sharp wind whipped fiercely against his aged face, his nightly mug of cider always gave him sufficient energy to brave the elements and walk the distance to his cottage at a sprightly pace. Once Marland wood was in sight, old Silas knew that there was only a little further to walk and then he could put a flame to the already laid log fire and thaw out with a glass of brandy before climbing into bed.

Silas had reached the gate to his little cottage and was just about to lift the latch, when he heard the sound of shuffling feet behind him. He felt his heart quicken and swung round to see the shadowy forms of three men approaching. Although one of the men remained in the shadows some distance from Silas, the other two brazenly approached him. The moonlight shone upon their rugged faces and Silas could see the menace in their eyes and knew perfectly well that they meant him harm.

Before Silas could say anything, one of the men roughly grabbed hold of him by his coat and demanded his money. Although Silas tried desperately to hide his fear, his aged voice trembled nervously and his whole body began to shake.

The man's grip on Silas's coat tightened and he repeated his demand for the old man to hand over his money.

Obviously eager to get it over with as quickly as possible, a second man threatened Silas, demanding the money from his pouch. He quickly snatched Silas Peet's gold watch and chain and suggested to his friends that they should take a look inside the old man's cottage.

Silas clumsily retrieved the pouch containing the day's takings from his pocket and gave it to the man, before pleading with them to now let him be.

Silas was not a particularly brave man, but he was not a coward either, and stood his ground when the men tried to force him into his cottage. "I've got nothing else to give you," he protested. "Take what you have and go."

It was then a third man who had for some reason kept his distance shouted from the shadows to let the old man be and go before someone else happened by and caught them.

The years had sharpened Silas Peet's senses, and without thinking he turned his head to look in the direction of the voice. "I know that voice," he blurted. "You're Tom Stafford's lad."

From that very moment Silas Peet's fate was sealed, and no amount of pleading would save him now.

The men were left with no alternative but to end the old man's life. One of them retrieved a knife from inside his jacket and with one powerful thrust, plunged it into Silas Peet's chest. He fell heavily to the ground where he lay still and silent.

Deciding now it would not be wise to enter the old man's cottage, the men fled into the night leaving Silas Peet's lifeless body lying in a pool of blood.

The old shoemaker's body was discovered by a farmer and his on early the following morning. Although Silas Peet was disliked by the majority of the locals, everyone was appalled and called for the perpetrators of the heinous crime to be brought to justice. News of Silas Peet's death quickly spread and rumours circulated that the old man's cottage had been ransacked and thousands of golden sovereigns stolen. Although this was untrue, it nonetheless fuelled the story of his murder. The locals feared for their own safety and were reluctant to venture out in the night, lest the same dreadful thing happen to them. As it was Christmas, little could be done to catch the murderers until the festivities were over. However, four days later a special court was convened in the village courtroom to discuss Silas Peet's murder, and after some deliberation, the local constabulary were ordered to interview Elizabeth Legg and her son Benjamin.

Although nobody really believed that Elizabeth Legg and her son had anything whatsoever to do with the shoemaker's murder, their home was searched as a matter of course. Everyone was shocked when the sovereigns the old man had given Benjamin were discovered, but as far as the law was concerned, it was now a fairly cut-and-dried case. Everyone was now certain that Silas Peet's apprentice had committed the heinous crime. As the old man was a known miser, the very suggestion that he actually gave three golden sovereigns to Benjamin Legg for Christmas was completely dismissed by everyone. The boy was arrested and taken to the village lockup until a trial had been arranged for two days later.

The boy's evidence in his own defence was also dismissed by the judge as "preposterous," and although the trial continued for a further five days, the jury's verdict was unanimous—GUILTY!

On the conclusion of the judge's summing up, the sentence was passed. "Benjamin Legg, you will be taken from here," were the judge's first solemn words, "to Kirkdale prison where you shall be hanged by the neck until you are dead."

"No! No!" interrupted Benjamin's mother. "My son is innocent. Please …"

Within moments, Benjamin Legg had been taken from the court, leaving his mother sobbing alone.

News of Benjamin's Legg's trial quickly spread far and wide, and had seemingly caught the attention of a notable barrister located in Grays Inn, London. Knowing the boy's mother would not have sufficient funds to consult counsel for the appeal, he contacted her by letter to offer his services free of charge.

The letter had no sooner arrived when Piers Gabriel arrived at her home to discuss his intentions. Such a high-profile barrister had never been known to give his services free of charge, and news of his visit quickly circulated through the village, giving rise to even more speculation. Piers Gabriel was a man of integrity and made it abundantly clear that he believed Elizabeth Legg's boy to be innocent and wanted justice to be done, proudly announcing that he had never lost a case in thirty-five years of practising law. "This is a travesty of justice!" he protested to Elizabeth Legg. "Even if it means compromising my own professional integrity, I promise you your boy will not hang."

Within five days, Piers Gabriel was standing in court before the same judge who had sentenced Benjamin Legg to death.

"It pains me to say it," he announced to the judge, "but Benjamin Legg's sentence proves beyond doubt that the law is in this case an ass."

The appeal court continued for less than an hour, and the judge was left with no alternative but to free Benjamin on the grounds that the evidence against him was not strong enough. To Elizabeth Legg's delight, her son walked from the court a free man.

No more than a week had gone by when the solicitors and acting executors for Silas Peet's will and last testament contacted the Legg family informing them, "We have news to your advantage." Silas Peet had left everything to his young apprentice, a legacy that amounted to over one million guineas cash, his shoemaker's shop, and the little cottage with three acres of land. Silas Peet's unfortunate demise had changed the Legg family's circumstances forever! They moved into his little cottage and young Benjamin continued to run Silas Peet's shoemaker's shop in the village, carrying on the trade to which the old shoemaker had devoted his entire life. Two months passed by when to their surprise they received a visit from Piers Gabriel.

"I need now to explain why it was so important for me to represent Benjamin." Piers Gabriel relaxed in the chair by the open log fire. "Although, I do fear you will find it quite difficult to believe what I am about to tell you."

Benjamin sat beside his mother on the leather settee and waited with bated breath.

"I have to say, Mrs. Legg, if you were to tell me what I am about to tell you, I would not believe you." His eyes moved from Elizabeth to Benjamin. "And I am not sure that you will believe me either."

"Mr. Gabriel," Elizabeth prompted, "please keep us in suspense no longer."

"Very well," He gave out a long sigh and sat forward in the chair. "I was working late in my chambers when my attention was caught by an elderly gentleman standing in front of my desk. As I had not heard him enter the room, I wondered where on earth he had come from. He told me he was Silas Peet and commenced to tell me the whole story from beginning to end."

Young Benjamin gasped when Piers Gabriel explained that Silas Peet's ghost had visited him to tell him that the boy was innocent of his murder. And after explaining to Piers Gabriel exactly what had happened, Silas Peet just disappeared before him.

"We are in a position to pay you for your services now, sir!" Benjamin said warmly.

"I have no need of your money, young man," he replied. "I am just so happy that justice has been done."

Piers Gabriel bade them both farewell, and Benjamin and his mother watched as Piers Gabriel slowly walked down the path and through the gate, pausing for a moment to look down at the spot where Silas Peet had met his death, even though nobody had actually told him where exactly the old man's murder had occurred. He then turned to nod his final farewell, and at that very moment Piers Gabriel disappeared completely into nothingness, just as he had said Silas Peet had done in front of him, leaving Benjamin and his mother standing on the doorstep, speechless and completely bewildered.

Not knowing exactly what to make of the ghostly occurrence, Elizabeth Legg wrote a letter to Grays Inn,

London, where Piers Gabriel allegedly had his chambers, enquiring if they could tell her anything whatsoever about him. Although it was two weeks before she received a reply, she was not in any way prepared for what came back. The letter from the clerk informed her that her son's benevolent barrister, Piers Gabriel, had in fact died in a tragic accident three years before, and that he was a well-liked and respected barrister who had also been known for his charitable work. Piers Gabriel was also a ghost and had returned from the grave to help young Benjamin Legg.

The Ghostly Child Minder

As a medium of thirty years plus, I have enough stories to fill several volumes, and although my wife Dolly is not a working medium, she has not gone without her own supernatural experiences—even as a child. Born Donna Maria Newkirk on Monday the 5th October 1964, she was destined to a life of unexplainable experiences from the very day she was born. In fact, they were so commonplace to the family, even her mother Winnie, a staunch Catholic, accepted them as being quite normal.

In the 1950s, Winnie Newkirk moved into a fairly large Victorian house in what had once been one of the more opulent areas of Liverpool, England. This was a grand, three-story house situated within walking distance of the two largest parks in the northwest of England. Although Winnie looked upon this as a completely new beginning, one of her main reasons for moving there was to be near her mother, who lived in the house opposite, and her sister Mary who lived just a few doors down the road.

The nanny to Winnie's three children also lived at the bottom of the road, so as far as she was concerned, the location was ideal, especially as her husband, Rocky, a Captain in the American Merchant Navy, spent months at a time away from home. The length of time Rocky spent away from home depended on the various wars in which America was involved. When he was away Winnie missed her husband very much, but at least she had her mother and sister to keep her company.

Sometime around 1958, what seemed like an almost idyllic life changed dramatically for Winnie Newkirk when she became quite ill. The doctor's diagnosis was that her health problems had been caused by the fact that the mother of three had had two of her children in quick succession. However, to exacerbate things, Winnie's sister, Mary, was diagnosed with leukaemia.

Within months, Mary had passed away and Winnie was devastated. Not too long after Mary's death, Winnie was diagnosed with tuberculosis and had to be admitted to a sanatorium for treatment. With two very young children to look after, she just did not know what to do. There seemed to be no alternative but to place them in a private residential nursery until she had fully recovered.

The problem seemed to be resolved, and Winnie Newkirk's run of bad luck seemed to be coming to an end. After eighteen months in the sanatorium, she was discharged with a clean bill of health, mostly. She was advised not to have any more children, but Winnie did become pregnant once again. And on Monday, 5th October 1964, she gave birth to a girl, Donna Maria.

Life for the Newkirk family could not have been better, and Winnie was now looking forward to a much brighter future.

One night Winnie was waiting for her husband, Rocky, to return home and her two children, Sheree, 10, and Denise, 9, were tucked up in bed, when Winnie saw a shadowy figure leaning over the banisters on the broad staircase. Thinking that her two mischievous daughters were misbehaving, she shouted up the stairs to them. "I will tell your father! Get to bed NOW!"

With no response from her children, Winnie went upstairs to see exactly what they were up to and was absolutely shocked to see them both still tucked up in bed and fast asleep. Although Winnie Newkirk was a staunch Catholic, she was also very down-to-earth and not one who frightened easily, and the eerie event was dismissed without further thought.

Other spooky goings-on began to occur in the Newkirk house over the following weeks, but Winnie was far too busy looking after her young family, so she just ignored it all.

The eerie phenomena started to occur fairly consistently over the months that followed, and although Winnie tried desperately to maintain some semblance of normality in the family, she began to feel a little afraid, if only for the safety of her children.

As baby Donna began to grow, Winnie frequently saw her young daughter talking to someone even though there was nobody else in the room. Peeping quietly at Donna through the slightly open door, Winnie was amazed to see that the conversation her little girl was having seemed to be two-way.

Although she tried to dismiss what her daughter was doing as childish imagination, she could not ignore other odd occurrences taking place around her young daughter. Winnie frequently witnessed the playpen unlock by itself, and she would be astounded as the whole thing rocked backwards and forwards, almost playfully, as if moved by some disembodied hand. Winnie also watched with amazement as the beads on the abacus attached to the playpen were pushed along one at a time, as though someone was teaching her little daughter to count.

Winnie would never have believed it had she not seen it with her own eyes. She could not ignore the ghostly goings-on around her daughter any longer, and although she was certain that whatever it was would not cause any harm, she still kept a vigilant eye on Donna.

Wherever young Donna was in the house, the ghostly figure of an elderly man dressed in Victorian clothes would also frequently be seen. In fact, the young child would often be heard giggling and talking to her invisible visitor. When asked who she was talking to, Donna would simply say, "The man over there."

As Winnie's child got older, she was able to describe the elderly man in greater detail and to explain to her mother exactly who he was. "He's my friend," she would announce matter-of-factly. "He looks after me and tells me stories."

As everyone in the family had seen Donna's ghostly friend at one time or another, he became accepted as one of the family. In fact, Winnie's daughter would become very distressed if for some reason she was away from him for longer than a day. The ghostly Victorian gentleman was extremely protective towards the young Donna, and as she grew older their relationship became stronger.

As well as the family, the man's ghostly appearances were also witnessed by some of Winnie's friends, and he became known as "Donna's ghostly child minder."

It was now clear to everyone that the ghost at the Newkirk's home was far more than a child's imaginary playmate and that over the years he had become Donna's invisible friend—a friend from another world—a friend from another time.

Winnie and Rocky Newkirk eventually decided it was time to move, so after giving it some consideration, they bought a house in a more select part of town. Although their older daughters were excited with the thought of moving, when they broke the news to Donna, by this time aged four years and six months old, she became so distressed that her parents even considered abandoning their plans to move. Nonetheless, a fresh start was needed and Winnie and Rocky decided to move.

Once all the furniture had been loaded into the removal van, young Donna looked through her father's car window as it pulled away from the house that been her parents' home for the past fifteen years for the very last time. She saw her Victorian friend staring sadly at her from the upstairs window, slowly raising his hand to wave goodbye for the very last time. Donna knew then that she would never see her friend ever again.

Sometime when Donna Newkirk was sixteen and sitting for exams, she had a vivid dream that she had returned to her old home to see her friend one more time. In the dream, he looked sad as he opened the front door to her and led Donna around the house she had loved and in which she had spent so many happy years with him. To her dismay everything was black and charred and she was overwhelmed with the smell of burning. She woke up from the dream feeling sad and depressed.

Donna never mentioned the dream to anyone, and one day her mother remarked to her sister-in-law that she would like to return to her old house to see what it was now like. She replied, "That would be impossible. It was burned to the ground and has now been completely demolished."

Although at the time she was deeply saddened by the news, Donna still remembers her Victorian ghostly baby minder with great affection and knows that he is still there, somewhere, looking after her.

The Reluctant Mourner

Since Jack Postlethwaite had died after a short illness twelve months ago, his wife Sarah had visited his grave every Sunday—hail, rain, or snow—without fail. Just tidying the grave and talking to her dead husband gave her some comfort. Although she had two loving and supportive daughters, Sarah was only too aware that they had their own lives to live, and now she had to make the best of hers, unfortunately without her husband, Jack. When the weather was good, Sarah would sometimes take a flask of tea and some sandwiches and sit by the grave on her husband's fishing chair that she always kept in the boot of the car, chatting away and telling him how her week had been. She was certain he could hear her, and it was only this comforting thought that kept her going. On each occasion she had visited the cemetery, she had noticed an elderly man standing over a grave a few rows away, staring sadly into space. Obviously missing his wife, Sarah had assumed, and although she frequently tried to engage the well-dressed man in conversation, he always seemed far too wrapped up in his own grief to even pass her the time of day. Sarah had always been the talkative type, and would talk to anyone, her husband always said. Even her daughters had always warned her about to talking to strangers, "especially in the cemetery, Mother." Sarah always dismissed their concerns, maintaining that she was now far too old to change and that it costs nothing to offer a kindly word to a person in need.

One beautiful autumnal Sunday afternoon, Sarah decided to pass the time of day to the gentleman, and although he appeared reluctant to engage in conversation, Sarah's persistence gave him no alternative.

"I'm so worried about my wife," he lamented almost incoherently. "Do you think she'll be alright?"

Sarah lowered her eyes to the sparse grave, noting the absence of any headstone or plaque bearing his wife's name. A bunch of beautiful red roses representing his love was all there was marking the spot where she was laid to rest.

"Of course she'll be alright," Sarah reassured him warmly. "God is good and always takes care of his own." She looked sympathetically at the sadness in the gentleman's eyes, and the pained expression on his face brought back her own grief when her husband, Jack had died. She placed a comforting hand on the man's shoulder and noticed he felt so cold. "You'll catch your death here," she said. "Would you like a cup of tea to warm you up? I've got a flask full."

The gentleman seemed to ignore Sarah and just continued to stare sadly at the grave.

"My name's Sarah," she said, trying desperately to break the heavy silence, and making every effort to put the man at ease. "What's your name?"

"Ted," he mumbled. "My wife's name is Irene."

"The pain will ease in time," she continued. "Believe me, I know."

The man turned to face Sarah, and a half smile slightly parted his lips.

"Thank you," he said quietly. "You are kind." He then turned and walked away without saying another word. Sarah watched him for a few moments before returning to her husband's grave.

All week Sarah found the gentleman constantly coming into her thoughts, hoping that she had helped him a little with what she had said. The following Sunday, as usual, she made her way to the cemetery, packing an extra cup and a few more sandwiches than usual in the hope of encouraging the gentleman to join her. It was a bright, clear day, and the cemetery was busier than usual, but there was no sign of the man. Instead Sarah noticed an elderly lady and a young woman standing at the grave, which to her surprise now had a new marble headstone. The two women were standing there proudly inspecting the new gravestone, and Sarah called, "It looks so much better now, doesn't it?"

The young woman looked at Sarah and smiled. "Yes, we're very pleased with it."

Sarah couldn't help but notice that the older of the two women looked quite sad and despondent, and so after securing her husband's chair in its usual place close to the grave, she walked over to have a closer look at the newly fitted gravestone.

"My name's Sarah—Sarah Postlethwaite," she said. "I visit my husband's grave every Sunday without fail. It's so quiet and peaceful here."

The oldest woman looked at Sarah. "Yes, it is. By the way, my name is Irene, and this is my daughter Barbara."

"Irene?" repeated Sarah quizzically, moving her eyes slowly to the grave. "You must be…" she stuttered, searching for the right thing to say, whilst her eyes read the newly engraved inscription on the headstone.

"Ted's wife," interrupted the woman, nodding sadly at the grave. "This is my husband's grave. He died six months ago."

"But…" Sarah stuttered again. "I…"

"You what?" asked the woman's daughter.

Sarah paused for a moment before allowing a smile to break across her lips. "Oh, nothing," she answered. "I must have been mistaken."

The Window that Looked into the Past

Moving into the quaint eighteenth-century cottage in a suburban English village was a dream come true for Astrid and Gareth Williams. As the couple shared the same likes and dislikes, the old house was exactly what they both wanted. They were now both looking forward to collecting furniture of more or less the same period of the house itself, and both agreed that they would be able to obtain a lot of the pieces from car boot sales and antique fairs. Astrid had an eye for interior design and Gareth was a keen do-it-yourself enthusiast, so between the two of them they were certain to create the perfect home. They desperately wanted to start a family, and had been trying unsuccessfully to have a baby for two years. They both agreed that the time was now right, and once they had settled into their new home, they were prepared to consider the options fertility treatment had to offer. They had been through quite a lot over the past couple of years, but now their life really was changing for the better.

It was 1983, and this was to be the couple's first Christmas in their new home. They were a stone's throw from the actual village and so in walking distance of the shops. It was beginning to snow and so they thought it a good idea to make their way to the supermarket to collect some groceries just in case it snowed heavier and they were unable to get out of the house.

"Best to be prepared!" Astrid was the practical one and always liked to cover all eventualities, whilst Gareth just took everything in his stride and would often leave things until the last minute. He was the first to admit that his wife was the boss and that she made all the decisions. Astrid would frequently shake her head in exasperation, and accuse her husband of "just making excuses for his come-day-go-day attitude to everything."

Upon arriving home from the supermarket, Gareth retrieved a bottle of chilled wine from the fridge, and then whilst his wife put the shopping away, he poured them both a glass of wine before placing two logs carefully on the open fire in preparation for a relaxing evening watching the television.

Although a fairly small cottage, it was structurally the same as it had been when it was first built, with a small feature garden in the front, and a communal cobbled yard at the rear. The picture-box windows had remained untouched and some of them still had the original distorted glass. This particular feature was something they both loved, and one of the windows in the front of the house cast an unusual light across the room on a sunny day. Astrid had heard some horror stories about the glass in these sorts of windows magnifying the sun and causing a fire. "There you go again!" Gareth shook his head and sighed teasingly. It was four p.m. and it was already going dark. They were both relaxing on the settee and as Gareth reached over to place another small log on the fire, he noticed an unusual light shining through the window. He went over to investigate and as he peered through the glass, he was amazed to see that it was no longer dark and snowing, but in fact was sunny and in the middle of the day. The puzzled look on his face prompted Astrid to quickly make her way over to the window—and she was amazed at what she could see. "What on earth is going on?"

They both rushed to the front door to take a look outside, but it was still going dark and now snowing quite heavily. Gareth scratched his head, and they both looked at each other, puzzled, before quickly making their way back to the window overlooking the street. To their surprise everything was now back to normal, with huge snowflakes now clinging to the picture-box window, and the glare of the streetlights glistening on the snow-covered glass. They both laughed and made their way back to the settee in front of the roaring fire. "That was so strange!" exclaimed Astrid. "I don't know what that was all about?"

"It must have been some sort of trick of the light," added Gareth logically, sipping his wine, and dismissing the whole occurrence. "A psychological phenomenon! It can happen. I think it's called Apophenia."

"Yeah, right!" Astrid wasn't too sure, but knew only too well what she had seen. Whatever it was, she thought to herself, the old house was warm and had obviously been well loved over the years. It was exactly what they had been looking for, and nothing was going to put her off it. In fact, she was prepared for anything—even ghosts!

The strange incident was soon forgotten as they spent the rest of Saturday evening relaxing in front of the television.

The following morning, Astrid made her way tiredly downstairs to make the breakfast for her husband, with the euphonic sounds of the nearby church bells pleasantly greeting her as she walked into the kitchen. The snow had fallen heavily in the night, so she went to the window to check the extent of the snowfall. She put her hand quickly to her mouth, unable to believe what she was seeing. Outside it was bright and sunny with no signs of any snow at all. Even more bizarrely, the road outside was completely unfamiliar and bore no resemblance to the road she knew—it had cobbles and there were no other buildings opposite, just a wide expanse of fields and an occasional sycamore tree strategically positioned along the pavement. As she watched, a horse-drawn carriage passed by, with the sound of the horse's hooves pounding the cobbles, echoing eerily across the road outside. Astrid was transfixed by the whole breathtaking experience, and all that she could do was just watch amazed as a bonneted lady in a long dress, obviously from a bygone age, crossed the road in front of her small cottage, completely unaware that she was being watched. Although fascinated, Astrid eventually managed to pull herself away from the window before dashing upstairs to fetch Gareth, who by now she was certain would be complaining that she had not made his breakfast. However, by the time they had come downstairs and were both peering through the window, the sight that now greeted them outside was back to normal, and a group of children were busily collecting armfuls of snow from the pavement for the snowman they had begun building against the wall on the other side of the road. Although Gareth had not seen what his wife had seen, he knew that she was not in the habit of embellishing or making things up. They discussed the whole thing at some length and eventually concluded that either the house must have some sort of supernatural aspect, or more logically that the window must be a portal directly to the past.

"Why though?" Gareth sat on the chair by the window, and thoughtfully placed his finger across his lips. "I believe that these things can happen, but why does it happen and why here?"

"I've no idea!" Astrid shook her head, bemused by the whole strange scenario. "I know one thing; we could sit here all day discussing it and never reach a logical conclusion."

As expected, the picture-box window overlooking the road at the front of the little cottage was the topic of conversation when their friends Eric and Linda Kirkham came for dinner the following night. Although their friends tried peering intently through the window, all they could see was the snow-covered road and the occasional car struggling to push its way precariously through the snow's frozen surface. Realising that their story was being politely dismissed, Astrid and Gareth decided to change the subject completely, and never again mentioned the window.

As the evening progressed, it had begun snowing again quite heavily, and it was decided that the couple should stay for the night. "You won't get a taxi in this." Gareth was adamant and knew exactly how bad the roads could be in such weather. "Besides, the spare room is warm and cosy, and you will be the first to stay in our new home."

The couples stayed up and talked until after one a.m., and surprisingly the conversation came back to the picture-box window. The four bottles of wine they had consumed made the phenomenon of the window seem much more plausible to their friends, who insisted that they should peer through it at least one more time before retiring for the night. But once again nothing out of the ordinary occurred, so, disappointed, they all decided to call it a night.

Astrid and Gareth accepted the phenomenon of their picture-box window as an integral part of their old cottage's character and decided from then on just to forget all about it if they could and get on with life. However, Astrid in particular was quietly intrigued with the window and would occasionally take a sly peep through it to experience life in their quaint little village in days gone by. Gareth was at work, and Astrid was sitting quietly in the lounge enjoying a cup of coffee before getting on with her usual daily chores when she heard someone singing. She swung her head quickly round to see an old lady sitting in a rocking chair in front of the window. It suddenly felt as though all the doors in the house had been opened as an icy chill passed through her whole body, and she felt as though someone had walked across her grave. She was speechless as she watched the old woman rocking backwards and forwards singing to herself, a song that was unfamiliar to Astrid's ears. The old woman was wearing a bonnet and old-fashioned clothes and had obviously lived in their cottage at some point in the past. Astrid was quite touched to think that the old woman still enjoyed passing her days contentedly in front of the window, rocking backwards and forwards and singing to herself as she watched life go by. Astrid was amazed that the apparition of the old woman in her lounge seemed as solid and tangible as everything else in the room, and wondered if she was aware she was being watched. No sooner had she thought this to herself when the old woman turned to face Astrid, and then, smiling at her, she slowly disappeared as though she had never been there at all. Astrid sat forward, and for a brief moment was unable to move. She knew now that the picture-box window was a portal to the past, as she and Gareth had thought—a portal to the old woman's world. She couldn't wait to tell her husband when he came home later that day, and he had no sooner set foot through the door when she excitedly blurted it all to him.

No more than a week had passed by when Astrid discovered she was pregnant. Although Gareth was quite sceptical, there was no doubt in Astrid's mind that the old woman's appearance had somehow played a part in making their dream come true—to have the baby they so badly wanted.

They never saw anything through the window ever again, and nine months later Astrid gave birth to a baby girl. She was now certain that this was just the beginning of a very happy life together.

FOUR

Poltergeists

It is the popular belief that poltergeists are in fact mischievous spirits, frequently malevolent and sometimes almost demonic. However, the poltergeist phenomenon is far more than a "mischievous spirit," and can take many different forms. Poltergeists can either be aggressive and quite malevolent, or just focuses of energy that are no more than quite mischievous and disruptive. Whatever force they manifest, poltergeists disrupt lives and cause misery and depression. They can ruin lives, initiate personality changes, and generally present as problematic situations and events, as detailed in the following stories.

Poltergeist in Paris

Interesting facts about poltergeists: Human fear, terror, and malevolence cause the release of minute particles of bioenergy into the atmosphere. These can persist for many years until finally transmuting into an immense powerful force that silently persists in the atmosphere, awaiting activation by an incarnate mind, usually a child. Although some dictionaries define a poltergeist as a "mischievous spirit," the majority of poltergeist phenomena are the result of focuses of dormant residual energy, initially produced by a heinous atrocity.

Over the years, I have investigated many alleged cases of malevolent possession, and I can honestly say that no two cases are ever the same. Many mediums mistakenly believe that their mediumistic skills qualify them to confront a malevolent force—this is far from the truth! Even though I have always had a special interest in poltergeist occurrences, there are occasions when I know I am out of my depth and simply have had to decline a request for help.

Primarily because of my interest in the psychology of the paranormal, over the years I have been invited to work with more than one Catholic priest, one of whom was Father Julian Calendro, whose speciality was exorcism. Julian was no ordinary priest; not only did he have a degree in psychology, but he was also a gifted sensitive with immense psychic abilities. Julian was born in New York and had been a priest at the Vatican in Rome for many years before moving to London, England. I had had the privilege of working with him on many cases, and I really was proud to think that he respected my abilities as a medium and valued my opinion, as well as thinking of me as his friend.

Julian Calendro had been contacted by a lady living in Paris and thought that the case would require the two of us. We spent over an hour chatting on the phone, and he explained the case to me in great detail.

Mariel Muccilia had been living in her luxurious apartment, within view of the Eiffel Tower, for three years. She had been quite happy living there alone with her Persian cat, Riana, until some unusual paranormal occurrences began some months before. Mariel Muccilia offered to pay us a fee plus all our expenses, if we would come to Paris to help her. She was in her mid-forties, and although she had never been married, she and her partner of four years were planning to buy a house together just outside of Paris. Her main concern was that, because of the paranormal occurrences, nobody would be interested in buying her apartment. News of the haunting had somehow leaked out, and it seemed as though the whole of Paris was talking about it. This eventually turned out not to be the case; it was simply a concern that the attractive lady was harbouring in her own very stressed and fearful mind.

It was a beautiful crisp but sunny spring day, and we arrived at the apartment just after lunchtime, just as Ms Muccilia was seeing her cleaner to the door. Although the smell of polish and air freshener overwhelmed us as we entered the spacious hallway, we both noticed an underlying odour that perhaps only Julian and I could discern. This was the smell of evil, usually indicative of a poltergeist presence or some other significant paranormal phenomena. I could feel goosebumps breaking out all over my flesh, and my heart began to beat like a drum inside my chest. This was before we had even begun to address whatever it was, and a sideways glance at Julian's face told me that he was obviously feeling the same. Although extremely beautiful and very refined, Mariel Muccilia could not hide the fatigue on her pale face, very often a symptom of poltergeist phenomena. If this is allowed to persist in a home, it gradually wears the inhabitants down until mental and physical health suffers. Whatever was happening was clearly taking its toll on Mariel, and something had to be done sooner rather than later.

We sat and talked over a cup of coffee and some hot croissants, with Julian doing most of the talking. I could see how he was approaching the subject with a carefully directed sequence of questions designed primarily to psychologically assess the well-spoken lady, whose English was word perfect. Julian's psychological profiling was a prerequisite, he said, for the work of an experienced exorcist. Although the furniture was perfectly and tastefully arranged, she assured us that every couple of days this would not be the case. Some disembodied force would cause chaos by throwing the heavy coffee table across the room and turning the Chesterfield settee and other items of furniture upside down. She went on to explain that these phe-nomena would usually be preceded by an overwhelming pungent smell, rather like a gent's urinal combined with rotting cabbage or decaying flesh, another indication that a poltergeist was present. As Julian's time was quite precious and his work schedule quite hectic, we could only remain in Paris for three days. This meant there was no time to waste. We arranged to return in the evening about nine p.m., and then we left for the local records office, located nearby.

As her apartment block was fairly old, Julian wanted to know something of its history. It did not take much in-vestigative work to discover that during the Second World War, the building had been commandeered by the Ger-man Gestapo to be used as their headquarters, and it was here that many individuals had been interrogated, tortured, and very often, murdered. Little wonder then, concluded Father Calendro, why poltergeist phenomena occurred in the woman's apartment.

Although at that point my friend did not allow me to be privy to what he was thinking, he seemed to know exactly what had to be done when we arrived back at the apartment later that night.

Julian Calendro explained to the attentive Ms. Muc-cilia that in his opinion the poltergeist phenomena were not produced by a so-called mischievous spirit, but by a concentration of malevolent energy that had been pro-duced by the heinous crimes perpetrated by the Gestapo in the building during the war. He went on to explain that whatever was producing the poltergeist activity had most probably lain dormant for many years, and that its aggressive force had probably been awakened by something very simple. Julian asked the woman if she could recall if anything in particular had happened that more or less coincided with the beginning of the poltergeist phenomena. After giving it some thought, she said that her father had died suddenly of a heart attack. "But surely it wouldn't be that?" she said. "It was such a sad time!"

Father Calendro looked at me and smiled, almost with a sense of achievement. In his opinion, that was exactly what had caused the poltergeist phenomena. My friend explained that it was the surge of emotion that had precipitated the dormant paranormal force, almost giving it a life of its own. Now part of the cause had been identified, we had to deal with the actual phenomena itself!

Although it had been established that the poltergeist activity was not caused by an actual disembodied entity, Father Calendro was adamant that it be dealt with as soon as possible, and that time was of the essence. My friend suggested to Mariel that to allow us to experience the full force of the poltergeist, we should stay in her apartment overnight. "Besides," he explained, "in order for me to eradicate the phenomena completely, I need to assess exactly what we are dealing with." Mariel had explained that the phenomena seemed to be confined to the lounge, so that's where we settled down for the night.

The hours seemed to drag slowly one into the other, with no sign of as much as a creaking floorboard. I could feel the anticipation building up like a volcano on the point of eruption, and around four a.m. things began to occur. The doors leading from the lounge began to violently vibrate followed by the heavy coffee table rocking from side to side, its momentum slowly becoming more and more aggressive. We could feel the Chesterfield settee shaking under us and the vilest odour suddenly wafted across the room. My friend explained that he needed it to reach a crescendo before commencing the exorcism ritual. A cacophony of groaning sounds throbbed across the room as a vaporous mist swirled about us, rather like a tornado moving across open terrain. A chair was thrown across the room, and the hands on the clock on the mantel moved backwards as its euphonic chimes pierced the stagnant air one after another. For one single moment it felt as though we were taking part in some surreal horror movie, with everything moving about us at some incredible speed. The phenomena persisted for a considerable time, and then with no prior warning everything suddenly stopped and silence descended. The stillness across the room was itself deafening, and my friend wasted no time. He retrieved an incense burner and sacred bell from his briefcase and immediately set about the process of purifying the atmosphere, concluding the ritual with a prayer in Latin. There was an immediate transformation in the atmosphere and the sweet fragrance of the incense somehow brought everything to a close. I could not believe that it was as simple as that, but I could tell by the look on Father Calendro's face that the ritual had been successful. Although extremely relieved, I could not help but feel that I was superfluous. I hadn't contributed anything at all and later had to admit that I had been a little frightened. "Me too!" grinned my friend. "I never know what to expect." I could not wait to bid Mariel farewell and make a hasty retreat.

That was fifteen years ago now, and as far as I know there were no further poltergeist occurrences at Ms. Muccilia's apartment.

Although Father Julian Calendro passed away a few years ago now, I have to say that I did learn more from him than anyone I have ever known.

The Relentless Poltergeist

I am often asked if anything ever frightens me, and if I'm perfectly honest, lots of things terrify me. For one thing, like most people, I do not like to be confronted with the unknown, and I do like to be prepared at all times. Although over the last thirty years I have investigated many different types of paranormal phenomena, I have always prided myself on being able to discriminate between what is genuine and what is not, and have also become known for my outspoken and straight-talking approach to the subject. The majority of laypersons tend to attribute every commonplace sound to the paranormal and very often think that I will drop everything to investigate their home. Many people have been disappointed over the years when I have either declined their invitation or disabused their enthusiasm by announcing that the bumps and creaks in their home had been produced by a noisy heating system or some other natural structural occurrences frequently experienced in old buildings. This said, I have always had a particular interest in the poltergeist phenomenon, but can usually tell whether or not it is genuine before accepting an invitation by the way the person describes the phenomena on the phone.

Some years ago, I answered the telephone to a rather nervous gentleman who obviously felt a little uncomfortable speaking to me. His reluctance to speak led me to suspect he had a genuine reason for contacting me. He had been given my office number by his daughter, who had been to a couple of my stage shows and had persuaded her sceptical father to contact me.

"I think there may be a poltergeist in one of my properties," he stuttered clumsily, occasionally coughing nervously to clear his throat. "It's been on the market for several years, and I'm desperate to sell it."

The man explained that he owned several properties, and the one in question was a three-story Victorian detached house set on one and half acres. Based on what he was telling me, I felt sure that the paranormal phenomena was genuine and I agreed to pay the house a visit the following morning, with the understanding that there could be no guarantees that anything could be done to resolve the problem. He agreed, but went on to warn me that two mediums who had called to the house previously had been violently sick and had to make a hasty retreat. Unperturbed, I said I would be there promptly at ten a.m., and then commenced to write the address on the pad beside the telephone.

As arranged, at ten o'clock on the dot, I had parked outside of the old house. Although it had obviously once been a magnificent family dwelling, the house had now fallen into disrepair and looked quite sad in comparison to the adjacent houses in the quiet suburban neighbourhood. I felt quite nervous and waited for a few moments to compose myself before approaching the house. It was a cold and blustery overcast day, the ideal ambience for such a paranormal investigation.

As I made my way along the meandering pathway, I noticed that the overgrown front garden was strewn with upturned oil drums, dismantled automobile parts, and other rubbish. In fact, it looked to all intents and purposes like a derelict, unlived-in house. I had no sooner lifted the heavy, tarnished brass knocker when the ornate oak door was opened by a well-dressed man in his mid-fifties who had apparently been watching me from the window. He looked quite nervous as he proffered a hand and introduced himself as Sam Godard before leading me into the hallway, where I was immediately overwhelmed with the pungent smell of damp and other fragrances usually associated with empty houses. I could see that the house had once been the home of a wealthy Victorian family and just wondered what secrets it held within the confines of its walls. It seemed quite peaceful—not at all like I expected. The impressive broad staircase still retained some of its dignity as it gradually wound its way up and then spread beneath a beautiful leaded window on the landing above. The leaded, coloured glass flowers were still intact, and the daylight filtered through the grimy glass and cast eerie shadowy shapes on the stairs. In fact, the old house was an ideal setting for a supernatural movie, complete with its eerie sounds and moving shadows.

Although the owner was keen for me to take a look in the rooms downstairs, for some reason I was drawn up the stairs to the landing beneath the colourful leaded glass window. The man left me to my own devices and allowed me to follow my curiosity, mesmerised by the shards of light filtering through the different coloured glass on the Victorian-crafted window. I had no sooner reached the first landing under the window, when I was overwhelmed with the familiar smell I always associate with poltergeists and related paranormal activity. I suddenly heard a piercing hissing sound, rather like faulty water pipes in an old house. All of a sudden I felt extremely nervous and jumpy, and for one moment was tempted to fetch the man from downstairs to escort me round the house. Shadows loomed in every corner, and every step I took seemed to echo through the house, before disappearing somewhere in the gloom.

Although I had not as yet experienced anything tangible, I was overcome with expectation and felt as though I was being watched by many disembodied eyes. I could feel my heart beating like a drum, and beads of cold perspiration had already begun to trickle down my face. The more nervous I became, the more I could feel a resounding throb in the surrounding air, causing me to feel slightly disorientated. I had experienced this before in other poltergeist investigations, so I knew something was warning me that something was about to occur. I tried desperately to ignore it and stood for a few moments, almost transfixed by the sunlight flickering through the coloured glass window when I heard a creaking sound and turned to see a blue vase standing on a table in the corner, vibrating fiercely for no reason whatsoever. I watched, amazed as the vase suddenly flew off the table and landed gently in an upright position on the floor in front of me. The table continued to vibrate and as its momentum increased, some invisible force took me by the shoulders before swinging me violently round to face the wall. I was unable to move and felt an icy chill pass through my whole body, and then without any warning at all, the same invisible force lifted me three inches from the floor before throwing me violently against the wall. Although all this took place within seconds, it was long enough to terrify me. Luckily I did not sustain any injuries, so I turned to make a hasty retreat down the stairs and saw that the owner of the house had been standing in the hallway below watching it all. "I think you need a drink," he said, shaking his head in disbelief. "Nothing like that has ever happened before."

He led me through a downstairs room towards the kitchen, where I was shocked to see it looked like a scene from World War Three, with broken chairs and upturned tables, and many other pieces of furniture strewn untidily across the room. I assumed that nobody could possibly have lived there until he told me that his daughter lived on the top floor with her husband and twelve-month-old baby. I couldn't believe what he told me, and then he showed me the rest of the house. There was devastation everywhere.

I was always taught not to allow any paranormal force to deter me, and that fear itself empowers any malevolent supernatural energy. I decided to continue my sojourn in the house and felt compelled to finish my investigation upstairs, only this time accompanied by the owner. Now, though, even he was afraid. "To be honest with you," he confessed, "I try to spend very little time in the house. I'm only here today to show you around." His words did not inspire confidence in me as he led me quickly from landing to landing, peering halfheartedly in each room along the shadowy corridor. If I'm honest, I wanted to be anywhere but in this house. And when we reached the apex of the house above the rooms where the owner's daughter actually lived, I noticed something in my peripheral vision and quickly swung round to see what it was. Although the room in which we had entered was completely empty, a light anomaly floated eerily across the ceiling and remained suspended for a short time in the corner of the room. This phenomenon seemed to be commonplace to the owner, who appeared nonchalant about it. We were both suddenly overwhelmed with the horrid smell I had experienced when I first entered the house, and as we moved further into the room, the door creaked and closed quickly behind us. Panicking, the owner of the house went to open the door, but I asked him not to. I was certain that the responsible entity (whoever or whatever that could be) was trying desperately to frighten us. It was then that I saw clairvoyantly a very old man standing by the door; he had deep-set menacing eyes, and a pale and drawn face. His feet were bare and dirty and he was wearing a Victorian nightshirt. He stood there for no more than a few seconds before disappearing. The temperature in the room dropped considerably, the windows rattled, and the door began to vibrate fiercely before being flung violently open again. We both made a hasty retreat to find ourselves thrown to the floor by some powerful invisible force. We began to shake with terror as we pulled ourselves quickly to our feet before continuing to dash downstairs, neither of us stopping until we had reached the marble mosaic floor at the bottom. As far as I was concerned, my sojourn in the house had well and truly come to an end, and somewhat confused I bade the man farewell and left.

As arranged, I later telephoned and spoke at the length to the owner, who was eager to know what I had thought and if I could help in any way. I explained that many years ago, an old man had been confined with a long illness to one of the attic rooms. The last few years of his life had been miserable and caused him to be extremely angry and bitter. He had in actual fact, died there alone. The energy created from his illness and the resentment he felt had contributed to the poltergeist activity. "Surely that's not all?" the owner answered. "All that chaos produced by an old and very sick man?"

During my visit to the house, I had also concluded that a young man had at some time hanged himself from the stairwell. All this and much more had culminated into an extremely aggressive force. I predicted that the owner would eventually sell the house to a German businessman and that the house would be demolished to make way for a new building.

Two years later, I learned from the owner's wife that that's exactly what happened. Today the old house has been replaced by a rest home for the elderly.

Upon hearing of my experiences at the old house, some years later I was invited by the owner of the rest home, who explained that the residents had complained that they were being disturbed every night by all sorts of unusual and very frightening ghostly phenomena.

The house may well have been demolished, but the disembodied force responsible for the poltergeist activity will never be destroyed and will persist forever.

Poltergeist at the Plaza Hotel

Of all the places to encounter a poltergeist and other paranormal activity, I would never have expected it at the famous Plaza Hotel in New York. Over the years, I have conducted workshops and seminars in various parts of the world, but there has been nowhere I have enjoyed working more than New York, where my wife and I always make it our business to combine work with pleasure and take in the sights of this fabulous city. Although we have always stayed in the Plaza Hotel, the very first time we stayed there was the most memorable from a paranormal point of view. We checked in to a luxurious suite overlooking Central Park, and after unpacking our suitcases, we sat on the balcony to imbibe the breathtaking ambience of New York. It was a beautiful autumnal afternoon and the hustle and bustle of New York life drifted up from below on the gentle fragrant air. I stepped from the balcony into the room to open a bottle of champagne and saw a dark vaporous mass in the far corner by the fireplace. Thinking that it was an optical illusion caused by me coming in from the glare of the afternoon sunlight into a fairly dark room, I rubbed my eyes, but the vaporous phenomenon was still there. I called my wife Dolly, and she confirmed that she could see it also. This phenomenon often occurs during the embryonic stages of a poltergeist or some other paranormal activity. Not what we would have expected in such a prestigious hotel. We stood watching the dark vaporous mass mesmerised by the way it swirled and turned before us. It remained there for at least ten minutes before quickly disappearing like a puff of smoke.

We thought no more about it and continued to enjoy our champagne before making our way downstairs to the restaurant for our evening meal. We returned two hours later to find our room in complete disarray, with the heavy coffee table turned upside down and a large vase from the mantel, although not broken, now lying on the floor on its side. Two heavy paintings that had previously been hanging perfectly straight were now crooked, and clothes hanging in the wardrobe were strewn untidily across the bedroom floor. Although there were no signs of a forced entry, my wife called reception to complain. Within moments, two young ladies were knocking on the door. They were clearly puzzled and assured us that none of the staff would have come into the room without our permission. They asked my wife to check our belongings to make sure nothing was missing. Dolly meticulously went through everything—even her handbag containing credit cards and cash had not been touched, nor her various items of jewellery. At that moment, I knew the mayhem had most certainly been caused by something paranormal. I was curious to know if anything like that had ever been reported in the room before, but the two young women appeared uncomfortable and made every effort to avoid my questions. "Well," said one of the young women reluctantly, "sort of. I've heard stories about a few unusual incidents in the room over the years. But I don't know too much about them. It was before I came to work here."

I could see there was little use in pursuing it any further, so I left it there. However, they did offer to move us to another room, but because we were now so tired, we declined their offer.

Although I never said anything to my wife, I did feel my first suspicions had been confirmed: a poltergeist of some sort had been responsible. What I could not understand was why did it occur in a hotel that boasted such patrons as movie stars, royalty, and the world of music?

We decided to have an early night, and our heads had no sooner touched our pillows when we were asleep. At three a.m., we both woke with a start. We could hear a woman screaming in the other room in our suite. The screaming was so loud that security came within moments to investigate. We allowed them to check the whole suite, but as expected, there was nobody there. Puzzled, the two men apologised and then left. We were now wide awake and sat up talking over a cup of coffee, not the best thing to drink in the early hours of the morning. By four a.m. we were ready for bed again, but before we could even snuggle down beneath the warm covers the bedroom door flung violently open and was followed by rapid percussive banging coming from the adjacent sitting room. We'd no sooner gone to investigate when the television came on by itself, with the volume turned to maximum, as if by some mischievous disembodied force. I was certain security would not believe us this time, and as expected within moments they were knocking on our door again.

The two burly security men listened to my explanation, but then politely warned me that I had to consider the other guests and keep the noise down. At our wits' end and not knowing what to do, we decided to sleep on the settee, and in the morning, as we were there for a whole week, we accepted their offer to move us to another suite.

There were no further occurrences and as planned we moved into another suite the first thing the following morning. Later on in the morning, one of the receptionists came to see us. She had worked there for some years and so was familiar with the historical facts of the suite we had moved from. She told us that there had been various complaints over the years about unusual phenomena, such as loud bangs and furniture moving, and said that it had been suggested that it was all linked to a suicide that occurred there many, many years ago. We have stayed at the Plaza on numerous occasions since then, always avoiding that suite, and never experienced anything like it since.

I concluded that this frightening phenomenon was in fact a clone ball, a focus of energy that is usually found in places of enjoyment, such as cinemas and theatres, etc. Although a comparatively new paranormal term, a clone ball is a focus of dormant energy created from particles of bioenergy that manifest from human enjoyment, happiness, and generally from having fun. Although clone balls usually slowly dissipate over the years, they can metamorphose into powerful mischievous and sometimes malevolent forces, causing havoc and mayhem. They can also be precipitated by suicide or murder or contact with a malevolent incarnate mind. After giving it some serious thought, I concluded that the poltergeist that occurred in our suite at the Plaza in New York was in fact a clone ball, an embryonic stage of a poltergeist.

Elizabeth Blunn

It was 2008, and I had just signed a twelve-month contract to appear on the popular television programme *Most Haunted* and was asked to be at the first location, a Victorian asylum in a remote area of North Wales in the UK on a bitterly cold winter afternoon. As we drove along the meandering driveway, in the distance the Gothic-style asylum looked like the set of a horror movie, with its tall chimneys silhouetted against the darkening October sky.

It had begun to snow and a biting wind blew fiercely from the surrounding hills. I had seen *Most Haunted* many times on television, and I was overcome with a mixture of excitement and nervousness. I had no idea what to expect, but just knew that I had to compose myself before filming began. This was to be an eight-day live show with the ominous title of "Eight Days of Evil," which made me feel quite uncomfortable. The presenters of the programme, the husband-and-wife team of Yvette Fielding and Karl Beattie, were known to sensationalise the programme by calling up the devil and other demonic forces. Fred Batt, the programme's demonologist, was in attendance, resplendent in his black demonologist's cape and looking very much like the actor Peter Cushing, known for his many roles in 1970s horror movies. In fact, the setting was ideal, and with so much history attached to the now dilapidated asylum, I was certain some paranormal phenomena were bound to occur. As it was to be a live broadcast an audience, two hundred *Most Haunted* enthusiasts, were allowed into the main hall to watch the show. As I was the guest medium for much of the eight days, I was to be seated on the stage with the presenter, British television celebrity, Paul Ross, brother of Jonathon Ross, the husband of screen writer, Jane Goldman. We were halfway through the week, and I was beginning to feel tired, very cold, and mentally drained. Paul was asking me if I'd felt or seen anything when I had taken a look around earlier before the show had begun that night. I'd been feeling quite uncomfortable since then and was suddenly overwhelmed with an extremely morbid feeling. "I saw a woman," I stuttered nervously, "a woman with a pale and very unfriendly face."

"She has obviously affected you, Billy," replied Paul Ross, with an almost dismissive voice. "Can you describe what she looked like?"

No sooner had he asked the question when I saw the woman standing behind him, her hands placed one over the other in front of her. Judging by her attire, I was certain she had been a matron in the asylum sometime in the nineteenth century. She was wearing a long Victorian-style black dress, and her shiny dark hair was pulled tightly back into a bun. She seemed to be totally focusing on me more than anyone else, with a stern almost alabaster face and piercing dark eyes. She said quite sternly, "I'm Elizabeth Blunn!" She repeated it over and over again. "My name is Elizabeth Blunn. My name is Elizabeth Blunn." I was engaged in conversation with Paul Ross, and yet I wanted to put my hands over my ears and run away, but I knew that I could not.

"Do you have a name for this woman?" Paul Ross almost goaded. "If you can see and her this woman, surely she has given her name."

"Elizabeth Blunn!" I blurted. "Her name is Elizabeth Blunn." At that point, I felt nauseated and felt as though I needed to find a toilet.

"Elizabeth Blunn!" Paul Ross repeated. "Very interesting."

At this point, we went to a commercial break and I went to join my wife who was sitting with some of the crew at the side of the hall. My stomach felt in turmoil and I was overwhelmed with a feeling of sickness.

It was then that my wife told me that she had felt sick more or less at the same time as me.

As a medium I have always regarded myself as quite disciplined, and have never been given to fanciful notions. But I couldn't get Elizabeth Blunn out of my head, and my wife could see that I was concerned about something and tried her best to reassure me. After the filming had been concluded, totally drained, we headed back to the hotel. The producers and crew all met in the bar for drinks and something to eat. My wife and I went to our room to change into something more comfortable, and then joined everyone in the bar. After a few drinks, I began to relax. During the evening I paid a visit to the toilet. It was now around two a.m. and I was the only one there. I was washing my hands and raised my head to glance in the mirror. Standing behind me was Elizabeth Blunn staring coldly at me. She had a look of venom in her eyes. I swung round to face her, and although she never stirred, some icy cold force flung me across the mosaic floor. I pulled myself to my feet and made a hasty retreat, leaving Elizabeth Blunn behind in the toilet. I returned to my wife and sat down beside her, ashen-faced and my heart pounding inside my chest. Concerned, and thinking that I was unwell, my wife took me to our room. Once there I explained exactly what had happened. As we spoke, although I couldn't see her, I just knew Elizabeth Blunn was still there. "Why me?" I asked my wife. I meant her no harm and, unlike the others on the programme, I treated everything with utmost respect. I felt so drained and knew that Elizabeth Blunn was sapping my energies. My wife suggested that we sleep with the light on, but even this began to flicker on and off. In fact, I have never been so pleased to see the morning sunlight shining through the window. I had the whole day to relax and recover from my frightening ordeal. There were still a couple of days of filming left, and I was dreading it.

The Live Show concluded on Halloween without another appearance from Elizabeth Blunn. I had never really experienced anything like it before, and I was puzzled why she had targeted me the way she did. Apart from telling me her name and indicating that she was a matron in the asylum, nothing else was known. However, I did get the strong feeling that she was a wicked lady and the perpetrator of cruel acts towards the asylum's inmates. Although I was relieved when filming at the Victorian Asylum was all over, Elizabeth Blunn had already decided that her contact with me was far from over. In fact, she visited me several times over the months that followed, until I eventually realised that she needed my help. She confessed to me that she had been the perpetrator of much cruelty at the Victorian asylum, and I could see that because she did not know she was dead, she had found it difficult to move into the light. Reluctantly, I helped her by making her realise that she was dead and that she was more or less earthbound. This done Elizabeth Blunn was finally able to find her way through the shadows of her own conscience, back home into that place of light.

Disturbing the Dead

Workmen involved in the refurbishment of a Victorian house, which had once been the home to a wealthy merchant and his family, encountered far more than they bargained for during the course of their work.

While they were clearing out the dimly lit basement, the two young men suddenly stopped when they heard disembodied wailing sounds echoing eerily through the darkness at the far end of the dilapidated basement. An icy chill accompanied the eerie, spine-chilling sounds, causing the two workmen to run frightened towards the exit, each one frantically pushing the other out of the way, and not stopping until they had reached the garden at the rear of the house.

"You both imagined it!" scoffed their boss. "It was probably the sound of the wind and nothing more!"

But the two young workmen refused to go back into the basement and chose instead to work with the other men on the top floor of the old house.

As the work on the house was quite extensive, over the following days the two young workmen forgot all about the ghostly sounds in the basement and just went about their tasks. A week had already passed by and more trades-men had moved in to help with the house's refurbishment. Jack Sedgely had decided to carry on working whilst the other men had broken for lunch. As he set about taking some measurements on the broad Victorian staircase, his attention was broken by the diminutive figure of an elderly lady standing on the landing at the top. For a moment, he didn't think anything of it and just thought she was a curious neighbour who perhaps had wandered in to have a look around.

She looked quite frail, and his main concern was that she would trip over the tools and other equipment that lay untidily on the stairs and do herself some serious harm. Jack smiled at the woman, half expecting her to say some-thing, but her deep-set eyes just stared at him, and her pale, lined face remained expressionless.

"You will be careful, won't you?" he said, making his way towards her to guide her safely down the stairs. But he had just reached out to take the old lady's arm when she disappeared right in front of him. "What the..." he gasped with fright, quickly taking hold of the banister to steady himself. "Where's she gone?"

Once Jack had composed himself, he decided to thoroughly search all the rooms on the top floor, but the old woman was nowhere to be found. He began to doubt his own senses, and the more he replayed the ghostly experience in his mind, the more confused he became. He had never believed in ghosts and had always dismissed anything to do with the paranormal as utter rubbish. This experience had completely unnerved him, and although he was quite a physically powerful man, he decided to make an excuse and take the rest of the day off.

The ghostly occurrences did not stop there. On the Friday night when all the workmen had put away all their tools and left for the weekend, the security guard was just about to inspect all the rooms before making the building secure for the weekend when he heard muffled voices and footsteps on the stairs.

He made his way quickly to the front of the house and saw a young couple ascending the stairs. He called out to them, but his voice just echoed through empty building. The couple seemed to be completely unaware of his presence and continued to make their way up the broad staircase, laughing as they went. Before the security guard reached the foot of the stairs to follow the couple, they both turned and grinned sardonically at him, before completely disappearing right before his eyes. The burly man was speechless and couldn't believe what had just happened. An eerie silence pervaded and, although all the doors and windows had been securely closed, an icy chill suddenly passed through the entire house. He froze to the spot when he heard muffled voices and giggling at the very top of the stairs. Although he did not scare easily, fear propelled him quickly along the hallway and through the front door, where he tried desperately to pull himself together. It was only after the workmen had discussed their individual experiences over a drink one night after work that they all agreed that the old house must surely be haunted and that something would have to be done before the work on it continued.

At that time in 2002, I was presenting my own television series titled *Secrets of the Paranormal*, on which I investigated various forms of paranormal phenomena, ranging from haunted houses to haunted people and their experiences. After seeing the programme, the owner of the house contacted me to see if I would come and take a look at the house with the possibility of including it in the programme and getting rid of the disembodied occurrences.

The house itself was one of many yellow-bricked Victorian dwellings along a suburban leafy road in what was once an extremely opulent area of Liverpool, England. This was where merchants, lawyers, and judges once lived, and although today all the houses had fallen into some disrepair, efforts were now being made to restore them all to their former glory, thereby giving some semblance of pride back to the community.

I arrived with a camera crew and my producer at the house just after five p.m. on the Friday, and while the cameras and lighting were being set up, the owner of the house showed me around. I asked him not to give me any prior information about the paranormal occurrences and to allow me to wander through the house by myself. In one of the attic rooms, I was suddenly overwhelmed with a strong sense of foreboding, and although I could hear the crew talking downstairs, as far as I was aware, I was now alone at the top of the house. All of a sudden, I felt a strong throbbing sensation though my whole body and began to shake uncontrollably. I had never experienced anything like that in all my life and I have to admit to feeling a little afraid. When my fear reached its crescendo, some powerful invisible force pushed me from behind, throwing me heavily to the floor. I decided to remain there and just moved my eyes from one side of the room to the other, but I could not see anything at all. As I pulled myself slowly to my feet, a pungent smell suddenly permeated the room—a mixture of urine and rotting cabbage, very often indicative of poltergeist activity. Although excited at the prospect of actually catching something tangible on camera, I decided to make a hasty retreat and join the others downstairs. The obvious look of terror on my face told them something had happened. I wanted to get on with the filming as soon as possible, and as arranged, we were joined by the two workmen who had had the first strange experience in the house. While they were talking to me, I saw a frail old lady standing in the doorway, her aged face and deep-set eyes looking extremely disturbed. She seemed to be gesturing me to follow her downstairs, but then gradually disappeared into nothingness.

One of the young workmen admitted he had experienced other phenomena in the house but didn't want to tell anyone for fear of been ridiculed. He had seen tools moving across the floor by themselves and had watched amazed as a heavy workbench levitated some distance into the air. These phenomena had obviously been produced by a poltergeist and not by a single disembodied energy. Poltergeist phenomena are nearly always accompanied by pungent smells similar to urine or rotting cabbage. These offensive smells permeated the whole house, making it clear to me what kind of paranormal activity was occurring. Dormant paranormal energy, or as Russian scientific researchers call it, "bio-plasmic" energy, can be so concentrated as to affect movement in the heaviest of objects. This sort of phenomenon is very often precipitated once it interacts with living entities, as in the case of the workmen refurbishing the house. The young couple who had previously been seen ascending the staircase by one of the workmen had apparently been seen by other workers. I concluded there must be a connection between them and the old woman, and only by researching records at the city library would we be able to throw some light on the ghostly visitors, thus solving the mystery once and for all. After some extensive research, our suspicions were confirmed.

Although nothing all that spectacular was actually caught on camera, we did manage to film unusual light anomalies drifting through the rubble in the basement.

Some weeks after the programme had aired, I was contacted by the house's owner, who wanted to give me some astonishing news. While a group of workmen were clearing years and years of rubble from the basement, they discovered the decomposed remains of a body, believed to be that of an elderly woman. Police investigations revealed that the woman had once lived in the house, and although it was impossible to determine the cause of death, they believed that her body had been there for at least fifty years. Further reports showed that a young couple had died in the house of a drug overdose sometime in the 1960s, during which time the house had been converted into apartments.

The mystery had been solved. Or had it?

The Ghosts of Parklea Manor

When I first met my wife, Dolly, she was the proud owner of a Victorian manor house in the suburbs of Liverpool, England. Although in somewhat of a dilapidated state, it did not take much imagination to see what it had once been like when it was the home to a wealthy merchant. In fact, the merchant who had lived at Parklea Manor had been an infamous slave trader, and it was known that he had kept slaves shackled to the cellar walls whilst waiting for a ship to convey them to other destinations. Liverpool was a thriving port during the early nineteenth century, and Parklea Manor was a stone's throw from the River Mersey, where the ships would collect the human contraband to be transported to the Americas. The damp cellars of Parklea Manor bore grim reminders of the terror and misery that had once been inflicted on the black slaves huddled together on the damp, cold floor, anxiously awaiting their fate. Shackles and chains still remained attached to the crumbling cellar walls, which led along a dark winding tunnel that meandered down to the nearby river, along which the black slaves would be led to and from ships moored nearby. The old house itself was a grim reminder of the slave trafficking that had once been one of the world's most lucrative trades. Dolly was desperate to sell the house and asked if I could possibly do something to restore some semblance of peace and order to it.

Parklea was one of several manor houses situated in Fulwood Park, a gated leafy suburban locale that stood as a reminder of the opulence of those days when Liverpool was a thriving port, and the wealthy lived within the confines of their own self-created, secure, and very private communities.

Once in Fulwood Park, the road meanders for a short distance before reaching the gates of Parklea Manor, which

I later learned was one of the most haunted houses in the UK.

Even though the original ornate gates along with their cast-iron railings had long since gone, little effort was required to see that the cracked and decaying walls of the old manor house once represented the finest architecture and wealth of those bygone Victorian days.

As I walked through the double oak doors into the spacious hallway that very first time, with its black and white mosaic marble floor, I immediately felt that I was being watched by many disembodied eyes.

The first night I spent in the house, I woke up in the early hours to the sound of chamber music coming from the now derelict ballroom situated in the west wing. I also saw women in long, flowing gowns making their way merrily down the broad staircase towards the wood-panelled drawing room at the front of the building. Dolly then drew my attention to the ghostly sound of young women giggling and chatting at the far end of the landing. It was three a.m. and neither of us could sleep, so Dolly suggested we should take a walk downstairs so I could experience for myself other unusual phenomena that often occurred in the dead of night.

Once downstairs, I was amazed to see clouds of cigar smoke spiralling above an old Chesterfield settee in what had once been the library, even though no one in the house had ever smoked. The cacophony of men talking and laughing also echoed eerily through the darkness.

Dolly explained that mischievous ghostly hands were frequently responsible for many items of jewellery going missing, only to mysteriously reappear sometime later in the most unlikely places.

I witnessed firsthand the dematerialisation of a large porcelain ornament that we later found lying in a pool of water in the cold cellar. Because it was so diverse, I felt certain that the telekinetic phenomena were produced primarily by a focus of poltergeist energy, the epicentre of which was the cellar.

I was amazed to witness doors opening and closing by themselves, and servant's bells ringing out even when they were no longer connected to any power source.

I stayed with Dolly (now my wife) for long periods at Parklea Manor up until the day it was finally sold to a property-development company, but to me the most frightening phenomena were the chilling sounds of the distressed cries of slaves echoing along the dark tunnels leading from the cellar to the nearby river, and the clanging of chains and the cracking of a whip piercing the cold heavy air. On numerous occasions, we both witnessed unusual light anomalies floating through the darkness, and a disembodied black man's hand frantically grabbing at the icy-cold air.

Once sold, the old house was eventually refurbished and turned into luxury apartments. Whilst inspecting the cellars before the house's refurbishment, two of the young developers ran away terrified when they saw the ghostly hand floating in front of them. They vowed never to set foot in the cellars ever again.

The refurbishment of Parklea Manor will not eradicate the ghostly and frightening phenomena that have been locked in the subtle fabric of the bricks and mortar, rather like images and sounds caught on an audio and videotape. Whatever happens to Parklea Manor in the future, its ghostly phenomena will persist forever.

Possessed by the Bitch of Belsen

In the majority of the cases I have worked on with Catholic priest Father Julian Calendro, I have to admit I did not actually do anything but observe. It was explained to me that in most of the cases, my presence as a medium was all that was required. As I learned a great deal from Julian Calendro, I really did not mind. Besides, I always regarded accompanying him as a great honour and privilege. One of the most frightening cases occurred when Julian asked me to go with him to the home of an elderly Jewish rabbi. We were to witness an extremely unusual case of possession involving a man in his mid-eighties, in which I was expected to use my mediumistic skills to determine what level of entity had taken control of him. Neither Julian nor I had ever heard of a person of this age being possessed. Today, I still have to admit that possession has never really interested me as I do feel that the subject is an extremely complex one, and a phenomenon that has many questionable facets. Although Father Julian also had a degree in psychology, we both agreed that an objective opinion was needed, so he invited a friend of his to join us. We were joined by twenty-nine-year-old Rebecca Forsythe, a newly qualified psychologist from London with a deep interest in metaphysics and the human psyche. Julian had known her parents for many years, and although she was highly qualified in the field of psychology, she also had a special interest in the neurological implications of mediumship. As far as I was concerned, she was exactly what we needed. We all met at the rabbi's very splendid home in one of the more select areas of Manchester, and his housekeeper took us into the library, where the elderly rabbi and a gentleman were waiting patiently for us. Rebecca and I were introduced to Rabbi Gould, and the gentleman was introduced to us as Hans Lubbermilt, a German now living in the northwest of England. Although he spoke excellent English, it was clear that Hans Lubbermilt wanted the rabbi to explain.

During World War II, Hans Lubbermilt had been a guard posted at the Bergen-Belsen Concentration Camp from 1943 to 1945, when it was liberated. It was here that he met Irma Grese, alias "The Bitch of Belsen," and a sadistic killer who had at one time been in charge of thirty thousand Jewish prisoners. Hans Lubbermilt had crossed her on more than one occasion when he made it clear to her he did not like the way she treated the Jewish inmates.

She frequently threatened to have him reprimanded if he did not stop interfering with her work. Hans Lubbermilt now believed he was being possessed by Irma Grese, and at the age of eighty-five, it was making the last years of his life extremely miserable. He had only been in his early forties when he was at Bergen-Belsen, and was able to see the evil in Grese's eyes. "It was clear to everyone that she enjoyed inflicting pain and killing men, women, and children." Lubbermilt was insistent that he was only doing his duty and had never participated in any cruel acts. As he was not tried of any war crimes, this much was clear. I could see that Hans Lubbermilt was tormented by the horrendous things he witnessed in that concentration camp. Rabbi Gould had known Lubbermilt for many years, and he was able to vouch for his sincerity. The aged German had even smuggled food and toiletries whenever he could to some of the inmates in Belsen.

Rebecca and Julian bombarded Lubbermilt with questions for over an hour, before his face began to twitch and then contort, and his entire body started to violently shake. Julian and Rebecca tried to constrain him, but he continued to shake and his hands locked in a painful spasm as his head suddenly slumped forward onto his chest. The violent shaking stopped, and we watched as every muscle in his aged body relaxed. At that moment, it looked as though the old man had stopped breathing, but then he raised his head and opened his eyes wide, an almost fiendish grin parting his narrow pale lips. A few moments elapsed before Hans Lubbermilt began to speak, the sound of the voice obviously not his, but that of a young woman. Although I could not understand the language, it was clear that whoever it was spoke with such anger and venom. Rabbi Gould translated as efficiently as he could, and it was quite clear to us all that she was cursing everybody in the room, and condemning those who had sentenced her to death. Julian asked if I was mediumistically aware of anything; but all that I could see was the shadowy form of a woman standing directly behind the seated Hans Lubbermilt. Rabbi Gould was finding it very difficult to repeat much of what was coming out of Hans Lubbermilt's mouth, and we could only guess why. The whole scenario continued for no longer than twenty minutes, although it seemed much longer. At its conclusion, Hans Lubbermilt's head just slumped forward onto his chest and remained there for another five minutes. After this time, the old man lifted his head, a look of complete disorientation on his aged and pale face as he mumbled his first incoherent words. It was clear that wherever Hans Lubbermilt had been for the last twenty minutes, he was now obviously back.

Rebecca questioned him further, and it was clear to Julian and me that she was not convinced that Hans Lubbermilt was possessed. She explained that in some cases of severe guilt, parts of the brain shuts down, allowing another, usually dormant part of the subconscious to take control.

"It is down to rods in the temporal lobe." She went on. "In my opinion, this was not so much a case of possession as it was a case of extreme guilt."

Her suggestion angered the old man, who slowly pulled himself to his feet. Making his way to the door, he turned to face Rabbi Gould. "I thank you for your help, my dear friend, but I do feel this is something I now have to deal with alone." Within seconds, Hans Lubbermilt had left the house, closing the door behind him.

The four of us discussed the phenomenon at length, and although the young psychologist disagreed, Rabbi Gould, Julian, and I had no doubt that Lubbermilt had been possessed. Although the disembodied entity had introduced herself as Irma Grese, we needed to investigate further before presenting our final diagnosis to Lubbermilt. However, several calls made by Rabbi Gould to the elderly man proved unsuccessful, and no more was heard of Hans Lubbermilt.

Over the years working as an investigative medium, I have learnt that whilst many people prefer to believe that they are living under the watchful eyes of angels, there is a minority who are quite content with the idea that they may be living a life looked upon by demons. The question must be posed: "Are evil individuals born evil, or do they possess inherent qualities that demonic forces recognise as being easy to influence?" Whatever the answer, nature will always conspire to lead you into a place in which your passions and desires may eventually be gratified. After all, Buddha once said: "You don't get what you want; you get what you are!"

The House that Nobody Loved

As a medium, I receive many requests to visit locations where paranormal activity has been reported. The majority of these cases have a rational explanation and are either the result of natural occurrences, such as a noisy heating system, or simply that the building is very tired and structurally unsound. However, occasionally I visit a genuine place where paranormal phenomena occur.

One such place was a sixteenth-century farm dwelling in the Roman town of Chester, in England about five miles from the city centre. A couple in their mid-seventies had been living there for the last seventeen years, ever since their two daughters, Jane and Sarah had married and both moved to the south of England, where they now ran a successful business together. The old farmhouse looked typical: gnarled wooden beams, thick sandstone walls, grey stone floors, open-log fires, and a wood-fuelled stove that was nearly as old as the house itself. It was clear to me that the old house was badly in need of repair; signs of damp were clearly apparent, as was that smell one usually associates with old country houses, mustiness and the pungent stench of decay. It was apparent that the roof had once leaked, leaving one of the walls and part of the ceiling stained with damp. The house's obvious neglect was not due to lack of finance, but more to the fact that the couple no longer cared. I was certain of this.

The lady of the house was now in poor health, and the man's mobility was greatly impaired by a very painful and crippling arthritic condition. My name had been passed to them by Father James O'Connell, an Irish priest I had met some years before. I had worked with Father James on numerous occasions when he invited me to take a look at an alleged haunted location or even speak to someone who claimed to be under psychic attack. "The devil is at work here, my son!" the elderly priest warned me on the conclusion of our phone conversation. I must admit, his statement did bother me. I knew only too well that Father James was not like other priests. In fact, it was his no-nonsense approach to the paranormal that I found quite endearing. He was a breath of fresh air and often a great joy to listen to.

The elderly couple was pale and obviously worn out from whatever paranormal activity was going on in their home. I had no sooner sat down when Father James arrived. I had no idea he was going to join me at the old house, but I gathered that he had come along because the elderly couple was not comfortable with the fact that I was a medium and had only agreed to have me there under great protest. They were staunch Catholics and had apparently donated a lot of money to their local church. Although extremely polite, it was obvious to me that they were not at all happy with my presence. However, as long as Father James was there too, they were prepared to tolerate me.

Father James gave me a guided tour of the old house, watching me intently for any signs that I had detected the source of the problem. Apart from the fact that I felt extremely uncomfortable, at that point I neither saw nor heard anything of a paranormal nature.

Father James eventually explained that whoever or whatever was responsible for the paranormal disturbance it was always preceded by a foul smelling stench, which was followed by telekinetic activity, during which items of furniture were thrown around the room, as if by some angry disembodied force. I had noticed the absence of ornaments and vases on the shelves and other surfaces, and it was now apparent why. Things of value had either been broken or put away for safekeeping, and some pieces of antique furniture had obviously been repaired.

So that I could witness the paranormal occurrences for myself, the couple invited Father James and me to stay for dinner.

Although I felt slightly intimidated by the immense pressure to almost perform, I knew there was something untoward in the house, and I just knew that things would occur while I was there.

The meal was eaten and the table was cleared and we all sat round the roaring log fire talking about anything but the old house's paranormal phenomena. It was the middle of November, and the wind was howling fiercely down the chimney. The ambience was just right as the flickering flames of the fire cast an eerie light across the dimly lit room. I needed my senses to remain sharp and so I declined the offer of a glass of wine, which was obviously a nightly ritual for my hosts. There was a momentary break in the conversation, and the lady of the house stifled a yawn and glanced at the old clock on the mantel as it chimed marking out the hour of 8:00 p.m. It was precisely at that moment that I heard a rumbling sound erupting from the ground below, even though I was informed that the house did not have a cellar. The deep, throbbing sound reached a deafening crescendo before shaking the entire house, rather like the violent eruption of a volcano or train passing nearby. It dissipated without warning and for a moment silence ensued. Father James watched me for a response but I was at a loss for words and all I could do was raise my brows.

I looked at our hosts, who were obviously used to such an occurrence, and the man just smiled as he leaned forward to place another small log on the fire. The silence soon came to an abrupt end as the door behind me flew violently open, causing both Father James and myself to spring to our feet almost in unison. I could see a dark cloudy mass move into the room, slamming the door fiercely behind it while throwing a small coffee table aggressively onto its side. The elderly couple scarcely stirred from their positions by the fire, although the woman did close her eyes in anguish. I could see that she was not so much afraid as she was worn out by it all. Whoever or whatever had come through the door appeared intent on making their presence felt by causing havoc to everything in its way. Father James gave the sign of the cross and began to do what he knew best—offer a prayer in Latin. As I expected, this had no effect on the aggressive phenomena, and the telekinetic display that followed continued for a further five minutes before finally abating into complete silence. Although quite used to it, the elderly couple were clearly disturbed by what was going on in their home.

The phenomena had only begun after an archaeological dig had begun in the field adjacent to the couple's farmhouse. Although they had in fact once owned an extensive part of the surrounding land, only one acre of it was still in their possession. Surprisingly this had been transformed into a beautifully landscaped garden, they said, cared for by their gardener of ten years.

I returned two days later to find Father James already there sipping a cup of tea and eating a digestive biscuit. Because of his wife's health, the elderly man made the decision to sell up and move to the south of England where both their daughters now lived with their families. Enquiries to the nearby archaeological dig by Father James revealed that there had been a small skirmish between Roman Legionnaires and local peasants, resulting in many fatalities. Many of the dead had been laid to rest where they fell, on the land that had previously been owned by the elderly couple. This, Father James and I had concluded, must surely be the reason for the paranormal occurrences. They, however, believed that the phenomena were produced by evil forces. However, I saw the phenomena not so much produced by evil as it was by unrest. I was certain that it was not the house itself that needed exorcising, but the sacred ground that now needed consecrating to allow the spirits of the dead to move on in peace. Because the house had been uncared for, it had somehow become a representation of the combined forces of those who had died on the adjacent field. I was certain that once the field itself had been blessed, even though archaeologists were still turning the earth over in search of more relics, the phenomena would cease! Father James carried out the ceremony and the phenomena never occurred again!

The elderly couple decided to remain in the house in which they had spent many happy years after all, and although they have both since passed away, according to Father James no further paranormal occurrences have been reported at the old farmhouse.

The Malevolent Woman

At her wits' end and not knowing what to do, medium Elsie Cotgrieve asked me if I would accompany her to a remote farmhouse she had been visiting for some months on the outskirts of Manchester in the UK. She explained that there was a great deal of poltergeist phenomena and that it was psychologically affecting the twelve-year-old daughter and her father. That's all Elsie wanted to tell me. "Come and see for yourself," she said wearily. "I've done all that I can."

As arranged I met Elsie and her husband, Jack, at the farmhouse. The surrounding farmland had been neglected and the house itself had been allowed to fall into disrepair. I'd never seen Elsie look so nervous as the door was opened by a sickly looking man in his mid-fifties. His face was ashen and drawn, and his eyes dead. He braved a smile as he proffered a greeting hand, which was limp and clammy, an indication to me that he was unwell. I had seen this look many times before in people who had been gradually worn down by a poltergeist. He beckoned us to follow him along the narrow, dimly lit hallway at the end of which light filtered in from a slightly open door. The smell of cigarette smoke almost took my breath away as the man stood aside to allow the three of us to enter the room where his wife was waiting for us. I was immediately taken aback when I saw a grossly overweight woman slouch on the settee, straight-faced and piercing dark eyes glaring quizzically at me. Before she spoke, she gestured to her husband in an almost demanding way to leave the room. He immediately obeyed her without so much as a word and left, closing the door behind him.

The woman went on to explain that she had been ill, and because of her weight was unable to go to bed. "I sleep here and have to stay day in and day out on the settee." She coughed loudly as she lit one cigarette after another, before stubbing one out on the ashtray full of cigarette ends and ash. The woman seemed more interested in telling us about her health problems than she was about the paranormal phenomena. She called for her daughter, who quickly came into the room like an obedient dog. She too was pale and thin and looked nervous as she stood in front of her mother. "Get me a drink!" she rudely demanded. "There should be some sherry left." The place was filthy, so I declined the offer of a cup of tea. The girl left the room quietly, like her father, without saying a word.

Elsie could see that I was becoming impatient with the woman's rudeness and near disregard for our presence. "Would you tell Billy what's been happening here?" she said sharply. "He's a very busy man."

The woman drew on her cigarette and glared derisively at me. "Are you a medium?" she snapped coldly. "A genuine medium?"

I decided to be as rude to her as she was to me and refused to answer. This angered her, and she moved her immensely overweight body uncomfortably on the settee, her face now red and twitching. Almost at the same time, her daughter entered the room clutching a mug full of sherry. The woman snatched it from the girl and immediately began to pour it into her mouth, gulping large mouthfuls at a time, pausing only to wipe her chin with the back of her hand, before gulping down the rest of the sherry. Her daughter stood there with her hands clasped nervously behind her back as though waiting for her mother's permission to leave. At that moment, the door began to shake violently before being pushed open by some incredible invisible force. Although the three of us turned to the door in amazement, the woman didn't stir, but simply handed her daughter the empty mug, demanding more sherry. A vile smell, like urine and rotting cabbage suddenly wafted across the room and the whole house began to tremble fiercely. Elsie Cotgrieve took her husband's arm to steady herself as the floor beneath us vibrated and every piece of furniture in the room shook violently. A chair by the dining table toppled over and the clock on the mantel began chiming and its hands turned crazily backwards. I noticed the girl was staring at her mother with a sheer look of fear across her pale face, and her mother was staring at me, grinning with mischief and evil in her eyes.

The cacophony of sound gradually abated, and as silence descended on the room, clairvoyantly I saw a man appear with long hair, resplendent in a white robe and clutching a long knife. I watched almost helplessly as he raised the knife and almost ceremonially slashed the young girl's throat. Although the man was not real, the woman's daughter quickly winced before placing her hand across her throat. I watched the man wipe the blade of the knife on his white robe before turning to face me. He grinned fiendishly before disappearing.

Although the girl was unhurt, I knew that the woman was responsible for poltergeist phenomena that occurred in the farmhouse. She was almost demonic and used her illness and what power she possessed to control her husband and daughter. We made our excuses to the woman and left. As we reached the front door the woman's husband appeared. He had an almost pleading look in his eyes as he thanked us for coming. I had no intention of returning and suggested to Elsie that she should decline any further help.

There was, however, a happy ending to this story. Elsie had suggested to the man to take his daughter and move away from the house. He did this and both he and his daughter began a new life in another town. The woman was diagnosed with schizophrenia and was hospitalised.

FIVE

Hauntings

If you were told that you were being taken to visit a haunted house, whether you believe in such things or not, your mind would have created its own ghosts and demons long before you had reached your destination. In the majority of cases, the mind is most certainly the common denominator. If you are seriously looking, every place with a history has its ghosts; some are quite demonstrative and can be seen without any great effort, whilst others are content to watch from the shadows in silence.

The House that Cried Blood

Just as audio and videotapes are coated with an electromagnetic substance that enables them to capture images and sounds for our enjoyment, so too is the electromagnetic atmosphere able to record images and sounds of days gone by. In fact, demolishing the location of the most horrific crimes does not in any way eradicate the cries of the victims, whose tales are locked forever in the memory of time. In this particular instance, although the house where two young children were slaughtered has now long since gone, their disembodied cries can still be heard echoing through the night.

As you meander down Binns Road in the Edge Lane area of Liverpool, England, now quite desolate and bearing no resemblance to the Binns Road of fifty years ago, those of a certain age will no doubt nostalgically recall the Meccano factory, the makers of Dinky Toys, Hornby train sets, and many other magical delights that once caused so much excitement for children on Christmas morning all over the world. Although the Meccano factory has long since gone, its memory still casts an immense shadow the full length of Binns Road. However, accompanying the ghosts of nostalgia, further along Binns Road, there is also the deep resonating throb of terror echoing across the desolate stretch of wasteland more or less opposite Crawford's Biscuit Factory. This is where the house that cried blood once stood, and where the most heinous crime was perpetrated by a psychologically deranged man. It was here in a tiny terraced cottage on one November afternoon in 1921, that a devoted father, traumatised by depression, slaughtered his two young children in a calculated and yet frenzied attack. He calmly led them upstairs and after callously slitting their throats, patiently awaited his wife's return from the nearby shops with their youngest child. The man was oblivious to the fact that the room in which he sat cradling the lifeless bodies of his two children was awash with blood. There was only one thing now on his mind, and that was to include his wife and young daughter in the macabre scenario, which he would then conclude by taking his own life.

However, his plan was thwarted when his wife returned home with a friend she had invited in for a cup of tea and to catch up on local gossip. Determined to complete the dastardly act, he waited quietly in the blood-drenched bedroom, rocking backwards and forwards in an attempt to stifle the insane rage that was throbbing inside his brain. The two women sat gossiping over tea and biscuits, completely unaware of the fact that the two young children were lying dead upstairs.

In the meantime, whilst the neighbour sipped her tea, blood had seeped through the ceiling and began dripping onto the woman's face and into her cup. The two women were immediately overcome with hysterics, and grabbing hold of the young child, hastily fled from the house, and within fifteen minutes the police had arrived. By the time the grisly scene had been discovered, the husband had slit his own throat and was lying with his two children, his life's blood pumping from the deep wound on his neck. The upstairs room was a veritable bloodbath—a macabre sight that reduced one of the policemen at the scene to tears.

The little house understandably stood empty for many years, and whoever did live there stayed for a very short time. Finally, sometime in the 1970s, it was let to a young newly married couple. By this time the community had more or less forgotten about the slaughter of the two children, and the young couple immediately set about giving the now tired cottage a complete makeover from top to bottom. Although the bloodstains on the ceiling had been neatly concealed, some brown marks were still visible, which the couple thought were just due to the general age and deterioration of the decor.

One morning, the young woman got up fairly early to make her husband a cup of tea and some toast and was horrified to see blood dripping from the ceiling and onto the table. Even after the couple had discovered what had actually taken place in their new home, they were determined not to allow the gruesome sight of the dripping blood to force them to leave. However, no matter how many times they painted the ceiling, the blood was relentless and always eventually seeped through. This phenomenon was soon to be accompanied by a cacophony of eerie gurgling sounds and the chilling sound of children screaming—echoing eerily through the house in the middle of the night. Finding it difficult to settle, the couple eventually admitted defeat and quickly vacated the house to move in with their parents until they had secured another home. From then on, everyone who lived in the terraced cottage experienced the same phenomena, right up until the very day it was demolished in the late 1970s. It became known locally as the "House that Cried Blood," and even though it has long since gone, many people have claimed to have heard the children's screams echoing down deserted Binns Road in the dead of night.

Since writing this story, I have since spoken to a gentleman who as a small boy actually lived in the cottage next door to the one in the above story. He remembers it well and recalled with deep sadness the funeral cortege, the horse-drawn hearse and the hundreds of mourners lining the street as the two small coffins were carried from the cottage.

In the dead of night, I have frequently visited the site where the house once stood and have heard for myself the disembodied screams of the murdered children that many have heard echoing eerily down Binns Road; innocent voices now trapped in time.

Haunted Plantation House

In 2003 I was commissioned by Sony to feature in a documentary to promote their new Playstation 2 game "Ghost Hunter," filmed on location in New Orleans and the Gulf of Mexico. Filming had been scheduled for three haunted locations; a plantation house in New Orleans, a haunted graveyard deep within the Louisiana swamps and a World

War II Battleship, now in a dry-dock museum in the Gulf of Mexico.

During the filming I was accompanied by New Orleans parapsychologist and author, Kalila Smith, whose extensive historical and paranormal knowledge of New Orleans meant that she was able to confirm all the information I gleaned at each location.

Filming began at a haunted plantation house in New Orleans. This spectacular timber-built house had been the home to many black slaves, some of whom had been beaten to death by the white overseer. As I expected it was extremely atmospheric, and as the camera crew and sound people were setting up their equipment, I wandered round the house alone to get the feeling of the place. As I made my way up the broad staircase, my hand running along the smooth oak banister, I was transported back through the years to when the house had been occupied by a wealthy merchant and his family. Goosebumps broke out all over my skin at the very thought of walking on the staircase that they had walked on for many years.

As I reached the top of the stairs, I came face to face with an elderly gentleman attired in breeches, thigh-length boots and a frock coat. He smiled and said hello in a broad Southern drawl. As the plantation house was visited by tourists from all over the world, I naturally assumed he was a tour guide and so thought nothing of it. However, no sooner had he spoken when he disappeared right before my eyes. I stopped in amazement and swung round to check behind me, unable to believe what I had just seen. I later discovered that whilst filming was going on, the plantation house was closed to visitors. But who was the man I had seen?

Filming was delayed when fully charged camera power packs were mysteriously drained and unusual light anomalies were seen moving along camera cables even when they were not connected to any power source. This was the production team's very first experience with the paranormal, so they were understandably spooked. The producer was clearly nervous and was eager to get the filming over with. A noticeable eerie feeling permeated the whole plantation house, and although it was in the middle of the summer, everyone experienced an icy cold feeling.

Taking advantage of the producer's suggested further twenty-minute break, I took another look around the house. It was now late afternoon and the sun had dipped on the horizon, causing eerie shadows to move from corner to corner around the old house. I was desperate to know its secrets and was sure the spirits of the past were silently watching curiously from their own quiet places.

I ventured into the dining room and glimpsed a little girl standing in the doorway, grinning mischievously at me. I thought she was the daughter of the caretaker, who had previously been wandering around the old house, but she was wearing a long white frilly dress and her hair was plaited and tied with two white ribbons. Although no more than ten years old, she looked quite malevolent and seemed to be trying to encourage me to follow her. Reluctantly, I followed her into the adjacent room, but she quickly swung round and began clawing at me with her hands, hissing and scowling, before disappearing into the moving afternoon shadows.

I was later told that the mischievous daughter of the plantation owner had been murdered by a black servant and that she haunted the house, perhaps in search of the person who took her life. I assumed that the man I had met at the top of the stairs was the little girl's father —perhaps looking for his daughter.

As we were leaving the plantation house at the conclusion of a long day's filming, the rocking chair on the porch began to rock by itself, backwards and forwards, the creaking of the aged wood echoing eerily through the darkness.

I for one was glad that it was over. Or was it?

Haunted Louisiana Graveyard

The small boat chugged its way through the murky waters of the Mississippi River, as the late afternoon sun, looking like a huge ball of fire, slowly dipped into the distant horizon, casting dancing shadows along our watery path. As if this wasn't frightening enough, hundreds of curious alligators watched the boat they had probably seen a hundred times before, pushing its way relentlessly forward, and for me a destination unknown. As with all the haunted locations, to ensure that I obtained no prior knowledge of its ghostly history, I was not told where we were heading.

We had been travelling for forty minutes when, without any warning the monotonous chug of the boat's engine changed momentum and the small craft began to move from its straight steady course through the stagnant water, to slowly begin pulling in to the bracken-covered bank. Although the Mississippi heat caused my clothes to stick to my body, I suddenly felt an icy chill pass through me when I saw a ghostly graveyard in the shadows of the overhanging trees. The producer informed us that we had to wait for nightfall before filming, to make it more atmospheric. She suggested that parapsycholoist Kalila Smith and I take a walk through the graveyard together in preparation for the investigation. We reluctantly wended our way along the meandering path in silence, intrigued by the crooked wooden crosses that marked each grave, and wondering who was buried there.

As night descended, the surrounding woodland seemed to come alive as a thousand disembodied voices chatted through the moonlit swamps, and unusual light anomalies floated eerily through the darkness before finally metamorphosing into ghostly forms. Apart from all the paranormal phenomena, snakes slithered menacingly through the undergrowth and huge spiders jumped across our path, making it so difficult to concentrate. I sensed that this was an extremely unlucky place to be. Everything went wrong.

Cameras and sound equipment developed unexplainable faults, and the producer was badly bitten by a plague of mosquitoes. After great effort on the part of the crew, everything was finally sorted and we were told to get into position.

The cameras had no sooner begun to roll when a huge white owl hovered approximately a metre above my head, its wings flapping almost noiselessly against the night air, before finally flying off into the darkness. I was certain this was a shamanic portent, and I was so shaken filming was suspended until I had gained my composure.

Even the young camera crew and producer were freaked by the whole experience and couldn't wait for the filming to end.

After I had given the information I had mediumistically gleaned, Kalila Smith revealed that Voodoo Queen Julia Brown had been taunted by the inhabitants of a Germanic farming community living in the swamps, and that she had cursed them. As a consequence, they were all killed by a freak hurricane. An elderly man and a young girl were the only ones to survive, but they mysteriously died sometime later in unrelated accidents.

We all breathed a long sigh of relief when filming in the swamps had come to an end, and we were once again chugging our way along the murky waters of the Mississippi back towards our hotel in New Orleans. And we still had another haunted location to visit the following day.

The Ghosts of a World War II Battleship

The following morning, after a considerably long drive, we reached our final haunted location in the Gulf of Mexico. This was a World War II battleship, now moored in dry dock as a museum piece and a grim reminder of the reality of the war and all those who lost their lives.

The battleship had been sunk by the Japanese with no survivors, and after being resurfaced, and undergoing extensive restoration, it was then opened as a tourist attraction. I was given a brief synopsis of its history but nothing whatsoever was revealed about any paranormal occurrences. However, with so many fatalities, I just knew there was bound to be a lot of paranormal phenomena. The ship had sustained a direct hit, and it was explained that the boilers had burst, killing all those working below decks. This was the first place we looked. Even the camera crew and producer saw shadowy figures moving frantically across the boiler room, as if trying to make a hasty retreat up the narrow steel stairway. We could hear disembodied cries echoing through the boiler room, and although in the middle of a very hot summer, it suddenly felt as though we were standing in a freezer. Kalila Smith's EMF meter went crazy, and as with previous filming, new camera batteries were mysteriously drained and the camera lenses zoomed in and out by themselves, without any help whatsoever from the camera men. It was quite bizarre to watch, and needless to say, the producer called "Cut" and suggested we move quickly to the upper deck to continue filming.

Before the cameras were set up again and ready to go, Kalila Smith and I walked across the main deck in front of the huge antiaircraft guns, whose boom, boom, boom echoed eerily inside my head. We both felt the pressure in the air dramatically change and saw a strange light suddenly spread across the deck. It was like watching a video replay of the battleship's last courageous hours fighting for its survival. We both stood mesmerised by the tumultuous roar and were overcome with the same fear that had driven the men during their last hours on the ship. We both glanced up and saw the figure of an officer looking down from an upper deck, angrily gesturing us to clear the deck and take cover. By the time filming resumed, we were both ashen-faced and drained. And we still had a few more hours of filming.

We travelled back to New Orleans in veritable silence, both replaying the whole experience in our heads, and neither knowing what to make of it. The World War II battleship still contained the fear, anger, and desperation of its last hours, and even though nearly seventy years have since passed by, the voices of those who lost their lives still echoed eerily through time. The ship and all the men who were tragically killed on it were still very much alive—perhaps locked in another dimension—another time.

The Gatekeeper

My office had received many reports of a ghostly hooded figure seen at dusk standing by the turnstile to one of the main cemeteries in Liverpool, England. I had a particular interest in the so-called "Gatekeeper" phenomenon, a mythical figure that is seen in church burial grounds and cemeteries. I am now far too long in the tooth, and far less naive than perhaps I was thirty years ago to believe the anecdotal accounts of phantoms without seeing them for myself. By all accounts, this was not just a mythical phantom but an actual entity that had been witnessed by far too many people to be the product of overactive imaginations. Now I had the opportunity to see it for myself. Strangely enough, the alleged "Gatekeeper" had been seen in two different locations, and more or less at the same time. To me, walking through a deserted cemetery is quite spooky at the best of times, never mind walking through it alone at dusk. I know only too well how the mind is able to create its own ghosts and demons, so I had to be prepared for all eventualities. After all, this was all in the name of research for my television series *Secrets*.

The phantom's appearances seemed to be cyclic and reports of its appearances made mostly in late January. Although I have been psychic since I was a child and a professional medium for now over thirty years, I still don't relish the prospect of being confronted by a hooded figure at dusk in a deserted cemetery. I considered my wife's suggestion of accompanying me, but I declined primarily because

I believed it was more likely to appear if it sensed that I was alone and more likely to be spooked by the whole thing.

I've never been one for ghost hunting gadgets, such as EMF meters or any other of the sophisticated devices used by many paranormal groups today. I leave all that sort of stuff to those who are interested in the more scientific approach to ghost hunting. So I decided to take a casual walk through the cemetery just before dusk. This particular cemetery is even quite scary in broad daylight. Although I had taken shortcuts through it since I was a child many, many times before, this time there was a strange light and a mist that hovered low over the uneven gravestones, eerily swirling and turning through the slowly descending darkness. I continued to make my way along the meandering path towards the turnstile at the far side of the cemetery, and was more than halfway there when I saw an indistinct figure ahead by the high wall. I first thought it was another person taking a shortcut through the cemetery, as so many people in Liverpool did. But as I watched with bated breath, the figure became more obscure before disappearing into the quickly fading light. I felt quite nervous and although I was of two minds to turn back, I knew this would defeat the whole object of the exercise. Within no more than five minutes, I had reached the turnstile where it was said the so-called "Gatekeeper" was to be seen every night watching all who entered the cemetery.

What I wanted to know was *why* it was there in the first place, and *what* the phantom was exactly. I stood no more than five yards from the turnstile and remained there for at least ten minutes. I had no intention of making my way back through the cemetery should my vigil turn out to be a waste of time, but to go through the turnstile. Although this meant taking the longest way home, for me it was preferable to walking back through the dark cemetery. I had no sooner thought this when a cloaked figure appeared no more than two yards in front of me, head bowed slightly with each hand pushed into the sleeves of its loose monastic garment. Its face was completely obscured by the shadows and although it never moved I felt transfixed by its presence. The monastic figure was slightly luminous and emitted a glow that became more intense with each passing moment, until as though in a puff of smoke, the Gatekeeper disappeared completely right before my eyes. Although I had no record of its appearance, at least now I had seen it with my own eyes.

There have been reports of a so-called Gatekeeper apparition in other cemeteries in many different parts of the world, and for some unknown reason, nearly always in late January.

So, next time you take a casual walk through the cemetery alone, do take care!

The Curse of the Archdeacon

I was invited to conduct a "Psychic Weekend" at the newly owned Hotel Commodore in Llandrindod, Wales, a picturesque and yet remote mountainous part of this beautiful country. The nineteenth-century hotel had once been the home of Archdeacon Henry de Winton, a bigoted and hypocritical man whom, it was said, had fathered thirteen children. The new proprietors of the hotel, Andrea Murdock and her husband Rohan took over in 2012. Faced with the arduous task of its extensive refurbishment, the couple soon learned that there was far more to the historical building than they knew. Even when there were few people staying in the hotel, the staff frequently saw shadowy forms moving down empty, dimly lit corridors on the fourth floor, and the temperature in the ballroom where bishops were once ordained, dropped dramatically to near freezing. The archdeacon's daughter died in the building at the age of ten months, and her ghostly cries frequently resounded through the darkness again on the fourth floor.

While we were there my wife and I were woken just after three a.m. by an icy-cold chill that suddenly permeated our room, even though the heating was on. We both sat bolt upright on the bed, and we could hear men's voices chattering and laughing in the en suite bathroom, even when we had been told there were very few guests in the hotel. As I went to investigate, the light in the bathroom turned on and off several times by itself and the sweet smell of incense wafted over me. We were then kept awake for some time by rapping sounds coming from inside the Victorian wardrobe and simultaneously from the wall behind the bed. When we did manage to settle down beneath the duvet, sometime after four a.m., totally exhausted, we were disturbed again when someone knocked loudly three times on the door. When I opened it, as expected, there was nobody there. And as our room was at the very end of the corridor, I had a clear view right to the very end.

As I had been told that the majority of rooms in the hotel were to be vacant until the following morning when coach parties were expected to check in, I knew our room was the only one occupied on that floor.

As the first medium ever to set foot in the Victorian Hotel, I was quite certain that Archdeacon Henry de Winton objected to my presence and that before I left, he was certain to show his displeasure even more.

We witnessed the newly installed elevator going up and down on its own accord, even after the staff had disconnected it from its power source. As my wife and I were making our way up the stairs late one night, a disembodied hand tried to push her backwards down the stairs, and had she not managed to quickly regain her balance, she would have sustained serious injury.

Before we left on the Sunday morning, the hotel's owner, Andrea Murdock, and her sister, Debbie, gave us a guided tour of the more remote and presently unused parts of the hotel, where they said a lot of paranormal activity occurred. At the uppermost part of the hotel, near the apex of the roof, still as yet to be refurbished, I became aware of wounded World War II soldiers and military nurses and was overcome with the anguish they themselves had felt. I was also conscious of nuns who I believed had frequented the building when the Archdeacon had actually lived there. This, according to Andrea, was highly unlikely, as the building was used primarily for the ordination of bishops and other members of the clergy.

During my sojourn somewhere at one of the upper floors I announced that a man had hanged himself from one of the extremely decorative and ornate banisters on the stairwell. Although at the time Andrea could not confirm any of the information I had given, she was eager to do some research and promised to email me on my return home.

As promised, first thing Monday morning Andrea emailed me to confirm that everything I had said was true. The hotel had in fact been used as a military hospital during both World Wars, and nuns stayed there in the the nineteenth century. A further revelation was that a young man had hanged himself, just as I had said.

We are returning to the hotel to do a further investigation later on in the year. This time however, we will be fully prepared for Archdeacon Henry de Winton.

The Paranormal Group Cursed by Evil

A prime example of evil by association is the Paranormal Ghost Hunting Group in New York that consisted of four young men and four young women, all sufficiently fascinated by the paranormal to inspire them to begin a group, just like their idols on a particular television programme. Although the young women believed totally in the paranormal, the four men were sceptical and just looked upon the group as a bit of fun with the opportunity to replicate what they had seen on television. An extremely eerie turn for the worst occurred when they did an "overnight vigil" in a house where two people had been brutally slaughtered in the latter part of the nineteenth century. It had been labelled the "Cursed house," and as a consequence it had always been sold considerably below the market price. Nobody had lived in the old house for longer than twelve months and, as it had been uninhabited now for five years, a date had been set for its demolition at the end of the year. Reports of poltergeist phenomena, as well as unearthly screams echoing through its empty spaces in the middle of the night had been reported, the very reason why the house had remained empty. It would seem that the house's ghostly inhabitants were determined that it should remain empty forever. This particular paranormal group had not been the first to visit the house, but as it was due for demolition, they would certainly now be the last. They had been given permission to remain in the house overnight, and armed with some of the most sophisticated ghost hunting equipment money could buy, the group of eight paranormal enthusiasts set up their cameras and other sophisticated equipment (and with an ample supply of wine and beer), prepared themselves for an interesting night. It was a particularly cold mid-November night. The light from a half moon filtered through the grime on the windows, casting eerie shadows on the walls and across the now bare floorboards. The house itself seemed to be alive with creaking doors and cold and draughty rooms, an ideal setting for ghost hunting. Although the majority of the group's members did not really expect to encounter anything of a paranormal nature, there was nonetheless an overwhelming feeling of anticipation amongst the eight.

Things began to occur around three a.m., with doors opening and closing by themselves and the cacophony of moaning sounds coming from the top of the stairs. Although nothing was actually caught on camera, each member of the group was satisfied that they had witnessed tangible paranormal phenomena. By the time the first signs of daybreak began to disperse the shadows through the empty house, each member of the group breathed a simultaneous sigh of relief, and enthusiastically unplugged the equipment in readiness to make a hasty retreat. Although the sceptics could not quite put a finger on the phenomena they witnessed, there were sufficient occurrences to make the group's most sceptical member reassess his lack of belief.

The group's overnight vigil somehow preceded a sequence of unlucky events. Although these could have been put down to "coincidence," what they later discovered left them in no doubt whatsoever that the old house was responsible, and they had all been cursed.

The group's leader, Mark Saddler had a near fatal accident at work, necessitating a two-month stay in hospital; Karen Fiske and her best friends Jodie Walsh and Liz Meaden were on their way home from a party when the taxi they were travelling in was hit by a bus, causing the three girls to be hospitalised for two weeks with the injuries they had sustained. Julie Robinson, also a member of the ghost hunting team, suddenly lost her job of five years. And then, to add insult to injury, she was badly beaten in broad daylight, when she resisted an attempt to mug her on the way home from the shops. The remaining three members of the group, Peter Slater, Karl Ronson, and David Robertson were all involved in a minibus accident, when the vehicle in which they were travelling careered off the road and rolled down a rocky embankment. Although the three friends only received minor injuries, the driver of the hired minibus was found to be over the legal limit of alcohol and received a six-month prison sentence for the offence. You would be forgiven for thinking it was all just some huge coincidence, but Peter Slater's curiosity led him to investigate the eerie phenomenon further, and he discovered something that transcended the realms of coincidence and caused each member of the group to completely abandon their interest in the paranormal.

Mark Saddler's accident at work had been caused by a careless work colleague Ken Pool, who later revealed that he and his family had once lived in the old house and had been forced to vacate it because of all the spooky occurrences.

The minibus in which Peter Slater, Karl Ronson, and David Robertson had been travelling had been driven by Ken Pool's sixty-four-year-old father.

The taxi in which Karen Fiske, Jodie Walsh, and Liz Meaden had been travelling was driven by Colin Pool, Ken Pool's older brother. In court, the perpetrator of Julie Robinson's mugging gave his name as Frank Pool, another brother of Ken Pool's.

Father Julian Calendro and myself did some research into the history of both the Pool family and the house itself. We discovered that the entire family had been well respected in the community, and could not therefore have been blamed in any way for the unusual occurrences. However, the house seemed to have many macabre secrets. Apart from the brutal murder of a young married couple, the house had also been the scene of a suicide of a young man aged fifteen years old. Further research carried out by Julian revealed that the house itself had been built on the site of an old cemetery. Julian concluded that this must have been the cause of so much malevolence, and that disrespect of the dead will always have its consequences. "For the protestations of the dead must always be obeyed," Julian always affirmed.

A malevolent force can never be destroyed, it can only be transmuted into a different form, from one condition to another. Disturbing it with disrespect, with a particular intent, can very often empower that malevolent force even more. It will live on forever.

The Lady of Light

Having been mediumistically inclined since I was a child, seeing so-called "dead" people was always commonplace to me. However, as a child I naively thought everyone was the same as me and could see exactly what I could see.

As a result of a childhood illness, I developed Bronchiectasis, an incurable lung disease, the prognosis of which was very bleak. My parents were told in no uncertain terms that their three-year-old son would not survive to see his twelfth birthday. Although the threat of death always hung like a dark cloud over me, I just knew that I was not going to die. I became extremely religious and from a very early age I wanted desperately to become a priest or even a monk. Little did I then know that my dream was viewed by my parents with some scepticism, for they were certain that it was a dream that would never come to fruition.

At the age of nine, because of the things I was saying to teachers and other children, the school nurse suggested to my parents that I should see a child psychologist. After the two-hour-long consultation, the soft-spoken lady psychologist's diagnosis was that, because of my health I was sensitive, insecure, and possessed an overactive imagination. She was in fact correct on all counts, but her prognosis that I would grow out of it was completely wrong. I did not!

Sometime when I was nine years old, one early December night I was playing ghosts and frightening my friend in the front room of our house. I was turning the light on and off, as kids do, and making ghostly wailing sounds, and trying desperately to frighten my friend Tommy. Suddenly the light refused to go on again. Even though I flicked the switch several times, the room still remained in darkness.

After several more anxious attempts to turn the light on again, a loud popping sound echoed through the darkness, and almost simultaneously an intense white light appeared on the wall at the other side of the room. We watched in amazement as the intense white light pulsated, before slowly metamorphosing into the figure of a lady attired in long robes of shimmering light.

My friend became so frightened that he ran to the door crying, pulling it frantically open and not stopping until he was out on the street.

I stood, mesmerised by the lady, now resplendent in golden robes of shimmering light and appearing as solid and tangible as any living person. She smiled and beckoned me to come close, but I decided that I should fetch my mother to witness the lady's presence.

I ran excitedly into the adjacent room where my mother, father, and aunt were sitting listening to the radio. "Our Lady is here!" I called almost in one breath. "Please come, quickly."

For some reason, I could never fathom why my father refused to come, but my mother and aunt were spellbound at what they saw, and all they could do was stand there, wide-eyed and speechless. My mother then thought the apparition had come to make her little boy better and suggested that I moved closer to the lady and touch her gown. I'd no sooner done so when the same loud popping sound that had brought the apparition there in the first place resounded once again through the darkness, and almost simultaneously the apparition disappeared and the light in the room came on again by itself.

I could tell by the look on my mother's and aunt's faces that they were totally bewildered and didn't know what to think of the unusual phenomenon. My mother then noticed a film of iridescent pink powder sprinkled across the spot where the lady had stood. Thinking that the perfumed powder may well have some significance she collected it, putting it in an empty pill bottle.

News of the apparition quickly spread around the close-knit community and came to the attention of the nuns in the local convent. Three nuns came to the house to pray at the spot where they believed the Virgin Mary had appeared to a sickly little boy. They told my mother that the Lady of

Light, as she had become known, had appeared to give the family strength in their time of need.

As it happened, the Lady of Light was portentous and preceded a sequence of disasters that were to befall my family. Some weeks later, my father nearly lost his life when a can of gasoline exploded in front of him, igniting his body like a ball of fire. My mother developed a serious thyroid condition and was hospitalised, my brother disappeared and was not seen for some years after. Then to add insult to injury, I fell ill with lobar pneumonia and very nearly died. Luckily for us all everything turned out well and we all survived.

Whether or not the Lady of Light was the Virgin Mary or some other Celestial Being, we shall never know. All that I can say is the memory of her appearance to me in the front room of my childhood home has remained with me all through my life.

Haunted Stable

In 1965 I was driving with a friend through Wales; it was around 9:15 p.m. and it was an extremely cold December night just before Christmas. The fuel gauge had been on empty for the last five miles and we desperately needed a gas station. This part of Wales was quite remote with nothing for miles except farmhouses and open fields. Our worst fear happened; the engine chugged a few times before stopping. The very last drop of fuel had been used. We both pushed the vehicle as close to the side of the road as we could, and then began walking down the dark country lane in search of a gas station, although we knew the chances of this were extremely slim. I didn't relish the idea of sleeping in the car overnight, particularly as extreme frost conditions had been forecast.

We'd walked for about half an hour without leaving the road our abandoned vehicle was on, when we met a smartly dressed young man. He was obviously not a farm-hand and looked as though he was making his way home after a night at the local pub. We explained what had happened, and after telling us the only gas station for miles closed at six p.m., he kindly invited us to stay the night with him. Very generous, we thought, until he informed us that he lived in a stable on the estate where he worked.

The stable was in fact only five minutes away and was located at the edge of a wooded area. The young man informed us that the stable hadn't been used for over fifty years and that he was only staying there until he found a place to live in the nearby town.

He led us to the far end of the empty stable the floor of which was strewn with old newspapers and then into a small enclosure where he said he lived. It wasn't until he lit the two oil lamps hanging strategically on the walls that we saw just how sparse his dwelling space actually was. There were no chairs or table and his bed consisted of several blankets and some pillows, which he kindly offered to share with us. "By the way," he said, in a matter-of-fact voice, "the stable is haunted by a horse that was beaten to death with chains by its owner nearly a hundred years ago."

We were intrigued and waited for him to elaborate. But all that he did was remove his jacket and loosen his tie before bedding down beneath the blankets for the night. Within moments he was asleep, leaving us slightly bewildered and wondering when the phantom horse would appear.

Neither of us wanted to sleep on the floor covered with blankets that did not look too clean, so we stood up for a while and waited. My friend remarked that it was now near midnight, and after spreading the blankets and pillows carefully on the floor we sat crossed-legged and chatted quietly so as not to disturb our host.

Approximately five minutes after midnight we heard the stable door open with a creak and the sound of horse's hooves clip-clopping into the empty stable on the other side of the wall that separated the stable from the tiny enclosure where we were sitting. We listened intently as the sudden sound of clanging chains echoed through the stable, followed by the neighing of the horse as it reared on its hind legs obviously with some distress. It was quite clear that our host was used to the ghostly sounds, as he did not stir. My friend and I opened the door slightly and peered out into the moonlit stable but all we could see were the old newspapers flying all over the place, as if scattered by some invisible disembodied force. We could still hear the chains clanging and the horse's horrific neighing, but the stable was absolutely empty. The temperature dropped dramatically and the phenomena persisted for over ten minutes, but our host still did not wake up. The tumultuous sound of the horse being beaten to death suddenly stopped, allowing silence to quickly return to the stable. We waited for a few hours before quietly leaving to spend the rest of the night in the car.

Some weeks later we were once again in the area and decided to visit the stable and perhaps see the guy who had been so kind to us. To our great surprise it wasn't there. We could see the foundations of where the stable had once been, but the stable itself had seemingly long since gone. We made a few enquiries at a nearby farm, only to be told that the stable had in fact been demolished over fifty years ago. It was further explained to us that a young farmhand had beaten his master's horse to death before hanging himself from a beam in the stable.

CONCLUSION

We may well question things we don't really understand, or dismiss the anecdotal accounts of other people's encounters with the dead. Mysterious tales will always abound about the victims of the most heinous crimes returning from the grave to ensure that justice be done, or about the dead whose screams pierce the darkness, in protest of their needless slaughter. The voices of the dead can always be heard, warning us, pleading with us, or perhaps just guiding us through the shadows of our own minds. Whatever you believe, you can rest assured that the dead are very much alive, watching and waiting…

Over the last thirty-five years, I think I can safely say that I have found myself in almost every paranormal situation imaginable. I have been thrown against a wall by a disembodied force, helped from dangerous situations by angelic beings, and even found myself face to face with an eighteenth-century coachman in one of the UK's oldest hostelries. I have even sat in a Catholic church having a long discussion with an elderly priest, whom I later found out had been dead for over twenty years.

Over the years I have learned as a medium and paranormal investigator never to dismiss anything as rubbish, for the simple fact is anything is possible.